Branch Lines of
Wiltshire

Branch
Lines of
Wiltshire

COLIN G. MAGGS

ALAN SUTTON

First published in the United Kingdom in 1992 by
Alan Sutton Publishing Ltd · Phoenix Mill · Stroud · Gloucestershire

First published in the United States of America in 1992 by
Alan Sutton Publishing Inc. · Wolfeboro Falls · NH 03896–0848

British Library Cataloguing in Publication Data

Maggs, Colin G.
Branch Lines of Wiltshire
I. Title
385.09423

ISBN 0–7509–0076–8

Library of Congress Cataloging in Publication Data applied for

Jacket photographs. Front: BR Standard class 4 2–6–0 No. 76028 at Collingbourne Kingston Halt with the Cheltenham to Southampton train on 15 April 1961. *Back:* D2187 at Malmesbury, shunting the daily pick-up goods, on 12 June 1962. Notice the red hay-making machinery awaiting departure. It was loaded by the hand-crane in the background.

Endpapers. Front: BR Standard class 4 2–6–0 No. 76028 leaving Collingbourne on 17 April 1961. *Back:* 45xx class 2–6–2T No. 5555 with a goods to Ludgershall on 17 April 1961.

Typeset in 9/10 Palatino.
Typesetting and origination by
Alan Sutton Publishing Limited.
Printed in Great Britain by
The Bath Press, Bath, Avon.

Contents

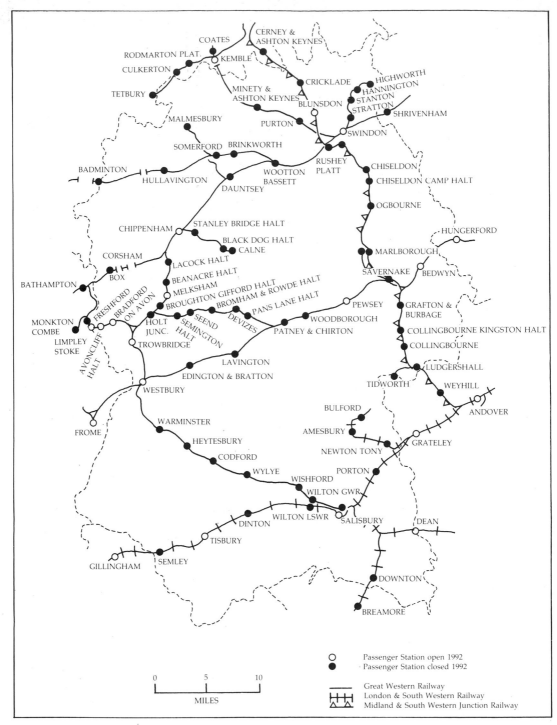

BRANCH LINES OF WILTSHIRE

Introduction

The railway map of Wiltshire is notable for the fact that it has three parallel main lines running east to west: the Great Western Railway London – Bristol; the GWR Reading – Westbury – Taunton; and the London and South Western Railway Waterloo – Exeter.

The first line in the county belonged to the GWR and opened to Hay Lane, 3 miles west of Swindon, in 1840, and then extended through Box tunnel to Bath and Bristol the following year.

The history of the other GWR main line was rather more complex as it was constructed piecemeal. The section from Reading to Hungerford was opened in 1847 as the Berks. & Hants. Railway, while the Hungerford to Patney section was built by the Berks. & Hants. Extension Railway in 1862. Further west, the Wilts., Somerset & Weymouth Railway had constructed a line from Westbury to Castle Cary in 1856. By the turn of the century the GWR had added these three lines to its empire. The company's critics claimed that the initials GWR stood for 'Great Way Round' and even its most ardent admirers had to admit that there was some truth in this statement. The area featured in the creation of a shorter route to the West when the GWR built a new stretch of line from Patney to Westbury in 1901, and from Castle Cary to Curry Rivel Junction, near Langport, in 1906, thus enabling trains to reach Taunton via Westbury, rather than via Bristol, saving twenty miles and more than twenty minutes.

In the meantime, a rival route to the West, constructed by the London & South Western Railway, was opened from Salisbury, which it had reached in 1847, to Gillingham in 1859 and through to Exeter the following year.

Three other main lines completed the chief features of the Wiltshire rail map: the Cheltenham & Great Western Union Railway, linking Swindon with Cheltenham, opened as far as Cirencester in 1841; the Wilts. Somerset & Weymouth Railway opened from Bathampton – Westbury – Salisbury in 1857, and its LSWR continuation from Salisbury to Southampton opened in 1847.

The third main line was the Bristol & South Wales Direct Railway, another of the GWR's short cuts. Before its opening, trains from Swindon to South Wales had to travel a rather circuitous route via Bristol, so a direct line was planned from Wootton Bassett to Patchway. This line was laid out for high speed running with maxium loads, no gradient being steeper than 1 in 300 and no curve sharper than 1 mile in radius. Considering that the line had to cross the Cotswolds, this was a fine achievement. The line opened in 1903.

The branch lines are described in order working from north to south.

Grateful thanks are due to John Hayward for checking and improving the text and captions.

Swindon to Highworth

The story of this branch began in 1875 when the Swindon & Highworth Light Railway Company's Act of Parliament received Royal Assent on 21 June. The directors ambitiously hoped to open the line nine months after work started, but by the summer of 1877, as less than a third of the cash had been subscribed by local people, the directors offered an inducement of half a crown (12½p) to anyone able to sell a £10 share. By February 1878 £12,000 of the £21,000 required had been subscribed.

The shareholders' problems were still not over as the company took a year to find a suitable contractor to carry out the work and it was February 1879 before one was found willing to take 850 shares in part payment.

The ceremony of cutting the first sod, which took place at Highworth on 6 March 1879, showed a certain lack of good organization as is shown by the *North Wilts. Herald* report:

> A small area had been roped off for the Ceremony and near this the Directors, Shareholders, etc., had been placed in a special area with the Ladies. Such was the attendance that this place quickly became full with results which can best be described as hilarious; the ropes gave way and the Dignitaries, Ladies and others fell into an undignified heap. The band, under Bandmaster Hawkins, continued to play unconcernedly.

The contractor started work a fortnight later. The following year the company had to raise a further £8,000, part of which was to pay for heavier track. This was because the GWR, which had undertaken to work the line, claimed that the permanent way laid was too light.

The inspection of the line on 5 March 1881, by Colonel William Yolland on behalf of the Board of Trade, brought further problems for the company. He found the signalling inadequate as facing points were not interlocked with each other and so could have permitted a careless signalman to set up conflicting movements; no lights were fitted to the level crossing gates; the depth of ballast was insufficient and there was no turntable at Highworth. Due to these shortcomings, he rightly refused to pass the line for opening to passenger traffic.

Arthur C. Pain, the company's engineer, abruptly left after meeting the directors on 4 May when they passed a vote of 'want of confidence in our engineer, Mr Pain'. The result of this sacking was that Pain lived up to his name and put forward claims on the company, the dispute being long and acrimonious.

As the company was heavily in debt, no money was available for the essential improvements required by the Board of Trade and extra capital was unlikely to be forthcoming. There was only one answer – to sell the line to the GWR.

In September 1881 the GWR offered £16,000 and agreed to take over the debenture debt. This offer only paid shareholders 24 per cent on the amount of their shares, but they were in no position to argue.

The GWR absorbed the Swindon & Highworth Light Railway by an Act of August

1882 and carried out the necessary improvements, though no turntable was installed as the line was to be worked by tank engines.

Following Major Francis Marindin's inspection on 30 April 1883, the ceremonial opening took place on 8 May when a train of six first-class saloons, four first-class compartment coaches and four brake vans left Highworth at 11 a.m. hauled by two engines. It arrived at Swindon at exactly 11.30 and returned to Highworth an hour later. The directors enjoyed a celebratory meal on their return to Highworth. The line opened to the public on the following day with five trains running in each direction.

A comparatively steep ruling gradient of 1 in 44 led to a direction being imposed that for safety reasons a goods train when shunting was to have two guards and a brake van placed on the line to prevent a runaway causing havoc. Also, owing to the light character of the branch's permanent way, only four-wheeled coupled engines could be run, though six-wheeled coupled engines would be allowed in an emergency, but no tender engines were permitted over the branch.

Latterly several industrial sidings opened at the Swindon end of the branch. One of the interesting features of the line was the Catsbrain House to Blunsdon footpath bridge, an original timber construction which was not demolished until the late 1960s. Beyond was Stanton Great Wood, a pheasant covert where it was not unknown for a lump of coal to be aimed at a bird from a passing locomotive! On one such occasion the men were unable to retrieve their prey on that journey, but stopped on the next. Just as the fireman was about to pick up his poachings, it was jerked away by the gamekeeper who had watched the whole episode. When questioned by the railway authorities, the footplatemen denied that coal had been misappropriated, but this was hard to accept when no less than five sackfuls were recovered from the lineside!

One driver 'learning the road' on the branch before taking over driving duties the following week, placed an inverted tin on a fence post as a marker to where he should apply the brakes before stopping at Cricklade Road level crossing. Unfortunately, when actually driving, he missed seeing the tin, and went through the crossing; the remains of the gates were left hanging on the buffer beam. Unluckily for him, leaves strewn across the track added to his problems as they caused the wheels to skid and so stopping was therefore less rapid than it might have been. Until 1928 this crossing had been manned, but then as an economy measure, its operating responsibility passed to the train crews, the fireman opening the gates and the guard closing them.

The Highworth branch was one of the last on the Great Western to be served by four-wheel passenger coaches. They had been retained as the modern 'B' sets were too tall for the branch loading gauge, a foot less than the GWR's standard restriction. The problem was easily overcome by setting the ventilators well down the roof side instead of near the top. Six of these special coaches were completed in February 1939, the 9 ft bogies being second-hand. The six coaches were made up of 2 brake composites, 2 thirds, 2 brake thirds.

On the outbreak of the Second World War this new stock disappeared, to be replaced by wooden-seated four-wheelers normally used on Welsh miners' trains. This proved to be only a temporary expedient and the special set duly returned.

Following the withdrawal of passenger services on 2 March 1953, goods and workmen's trains continued running until complete closure, except for a mile of line from Highworth Junction, on 6 August 1962. One unusual feature of the workmen's trains was that latterly they were hauled by a class 03 diesel-mechanical locomotive, only normally used for short-haul goods trains or shunting and rarely seen drawing passenger coaches.

The truncated branch is still used by freight wagons to and from industrial premises: Jack Dean Oils Ltd; Cooper Metals; Ministry of Defence (Army); and the Austin Rover Group.

3

KEY TO ALL LARGE SCALE MAPS

———————— Great Western Railway

⊦⊦⊦⊦⊦⊦⊦⊦ London & South Western Railway

△△△△△△ Midland & South Western Junction Railway

— — — — — — Military Railway

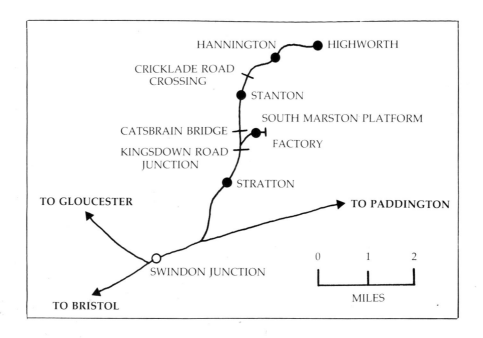

4

The evening milk train at Highworth headed by an open-back 0–4–2T. The photographer is receiving more attention than the train. The extension of the station building nearest the camera bears the notice 'Highworth Ground Frame' and the hole beneath the platform allows the exit of signal wires and point rodding.

Author's Collection

A general view of the simple terminus at Highworth, showing the timber-built goods shed and the passenger station beyond. The loading gauge is unusual, as due to the height restriction imposed on the branch, it has a flat, instead of rounded, top.

Lens of Sutton

D2195 has arrived at Highworth with the early evening workmen's train from Swindon Junction. This type of locomotive was very rare on passenger trains, generally being reserved for local goods trains and shunting. The coaches are special Highworth Branch stock: Brake Compo W6831W and third-class compartment W1238W, both new in 1939.

18.6.62   Hugh Ballantyne

1366 class 0–6–0PT No. 1366 at Highworth with an enthusiasts' special.

M.E.J. Deane

Highworth from the terminal end of the platform. The nearest building is the parcels office. The platform is paved with diamond-patterned blue brick. 58xx class 0–4–2T No. 5800 stands in the shunting spur. Below, the line to Swindon can be seen descending at a gradient of 1 in 44.

Trevor J. Saunders

58xx class 0–4–2T No. 5800 at Hannington heading a short freight train. The signal-box at the far end of the station building closed on 27 June 1910 and was replaced by two ground frames. In this view the track appears rather overgrown.

1958   Trevor J. Saunders

The permanent way gang at Hannington with their pump trolley. Pushing the bars up and down moved a crank, thus turning the wheels. Such a vehicle enabled men and their tools to be cheaply moved to their working site. The siding curving right looks like a hay field.

1958   Trevor J. Saunders

58xx class 0–4–2T No. 5800 at Stanton.

1958   Trevor J. Saunders

D2195 approaching Hannington with the evening workmen's train from Swindon Junction. The roof ventilators of the special Highworth Branch stock appear well below the apex of the roof in this view.

18.6.62   Hugh Ballantyne

Dated 24th March, 1880.

THE SWINDON AND HIGHWORTH
LIGHT RAILWAY COMPANY
JOHN DREW HIGGINS Esquire
AND JOHN CRIER Esquire

AND

THE GREAT WESTERN RAILWAY
COMPANY ,

Agreement.

R. R. NELSON,
Eastbourne Terrace,
Paddington.

Waterlow & Sons Limited, Printers, London Wall, London.

Cover of Agreement dated 24 March 1880 between the Swindon & Highworth Light Railway Co., John Higgins and John Crier.

D.J. Hyde Collection

No. 5800 about to pass below the Catsbrain House to Blunsdon footpath bridge. Built of timber, it rested on stone abutments, the right-hand one of which has a serious crack.

1958   Trevor J. Saunders

View of Kingsdown Road signal-box from the cab of No. 5800. The line to Highworth is on the left, while the branch to South Marston Platform and the Vickers Armstrong factory is on the right.

Trevor J. Saunders

South Marston Platform used by workers to and from the Vickers Armstrong factory, the entrance to which is under the bridge, on the left. In this view, the sidings are rather overgrown.

1958   Trevor J. Saunders

Stratton goods yard which did a good trade in coal. In this picture the 3-ton hand crane is the main feature, while to the right is a small goods shed. Beyond is the passenger platform with a pagoda-type parcels office and waiting room on its right.

October 1966   D.J. Hyde

Cricklade to Ludgershall

Although the Midland & South Western Junction Railway aimed at being a principal main line, for much of its history it was really only a local branch.

In 1846 Robert Stephenson, son of the famous George, promoted the Manchester & Southampton Direct Railway running from an existing line at Cheltenham through Swindon and Marlborough to Southampton. His basic thinking was sound, for it was through routes, rather than local lines, which paid the best dividends. However, the project was aborted as its bill was rejected in the House of Lords when the GWR promised to build a line from Basingstoke to Oxford facilitating north to south communication by an alternative route.

Stephenson's idea was not entirely forgotten and efforts were still made to connect Cheltenham with the south coast. The first part of the through route to be opened was the Marlborough Railway (see p. 44), opened from Savernake in 1860 and worked by the Great Western.

In 1872 local landowners projected a railway from Swindon to Andover linking the GWR with the London and South Western Railway. The Swindon, Marlborough & Andover Railway as it was called, received its Act on 21 July 1873. The line was to be built in two parts: from Swindon to Marlborough, and from Savernake to Andover, trains having running powers over the intervening Marlborough Railway.

The Swindon, Marlborough & Andover Railway directors realized that insufficient capital was available to construct the whole line and so decided to complete the Marlborough to Swindon section first, this being opened on 27 July 1881, though the SMAR's first fare-paying passengers had actually been carried on the previous day. The special carried about eighty boys from Marlborough College on the first leg of their journey home. (Marlburians soon used their ingenuity to give the railway the nickname 'Turnover Swindle'.)

Work continued on the southern section of the SMAR and this was ready for inspection by Major Marindin on 21 March 1882. At 11 a.m. a special train consisting of two composite coaches, a guard's van and four or five goods vans laden with stores and drawn by 0–4–4T No. 4, left Swindon. The points and signals at the junction with the GWR's Marlborough branch at Marlborough were inspected first. Steam was shut off on No. 4 and a Great Western pilot engine coupled in front for the trip to Wolfhall Junction over the Marlborough branch and the Berks. & Hants. Extension Railway, the greatest care being taken by GWR officials that the SMAR engine did not actually steam over their road as the running agreement had yet to be signed. Savernake brought an hour's delay as the junction points had been spiked. Points and bridges on the southern section of the SMAR were tested and Ludgershall reached at 3 p.m. where a stop was made for lunch. A heavy storm of snow and sleet made the inspection party's position on the front of the engine unpleasant. Andover station was reached just after 6 p.m.

In his report Marindin said that the GWR station at Savernake was incapable of taking further traffic and he also required several improvements elsewhere before he felt that the line could be safely opened to the public travelling from Marlborough to Andover.

Meanwhile the SMAR directors had to decide whether to allow their officials at the various stations between Savernake and Andover to remain unemployed, as some of them had been for over six weeks, or whether they should pick up a few crumbs by opening to local traffic. They decided to open the line from Grafton to Andover. The first train left Grafton at 7. 30 a.m. on 1 May. It did not carry many passengers as traffic was necessarily local until the gap of one and a half miles could be closed, but, including the short road journey from Savernake to Grafton, the distance from Swindon to Andover by rail was shortened by forty miles.

It was intended to start a through service from Swindon to Andover by running horse brakes or omnibuses between Marlborough and Grafton, but later this was thought inexpedient. As the railway officials themselves had difficulty in travelling between the two sections, the Traffic Manager appealed for a horse and trap to be provided. In the first half of the year the SMAR carried 1,041 first-class, 4,282 second-class and 43,084 third-class passengers in addition to 9 season ticket holders. Eventually the Board of Trade requirements were carried out at Savernake and the SMAR was able to run through trains between Swindon, Andover and Southampton on 5 February 1883.

It was still felt that this scheme was not really complete and that a company should be promoted to build an extension from the SMAR at Swindon to the Midland Railway at Cheltenham and thus create a new through route to the south.

The Swindon & Cheltenham Extension Railway, as it was called, obtained its necessary Act in 1881 giving powers to build a line from a junction with the SMAR at Rushey Platt, Swindon, to a junction with the Banbury & Cheltenham Railway at Andoversford over which it had running powers to Cheltenham itself. The SCER encountered problems with the GWR which had leased the rival Didcot, Newbury & Southampton Railway and was determined to prevent rival north to south competition. The SCER offered to pay £210 for an easement to cross the GWR's Cheltenham line near Moredon as the Act authorized, but the GWR countered this by invoking the Land Clauses Act of 1845 which provided that a company could not take land until the whole of its capital was subscribed. The SCER appealed as the intention of the 1845 Act was to protect a landowner against having his property taken from him by a railway when there was a probability that it would not be built. The Master of the Rolls gave judgement in favour of the SCER, the GWR's appeal to the House of Lords being rejected.

The junction between the SMAR and the SCER at Rushey Platt was inspected by Colonel F.H. Rich on 9 September 1883 when he found that one lever in the signal-box needed interlocking and the permanent way required repacking. It was re-inspected and passed on 12 October 1883, goods traffic running to Cirencester on 1 November, but passenger traffic could not start until the 13 miles to Cirencester had been inspected. This Major Marindin did on 27 and 28 November. He reported that the works were 'well and substantially constructed', but that on the day of inspection, wet weather had caused a slip in the embankment near Wootton Bassett Road at the point where chalk and clay soils met. Because of this fault, he could not pass the line for passenger traffic. Overed Watson, the contractor, said that in the four months from September to December more rain had fallen than for fifty years during the same period. He added that of the opposition, GWR, landowners and the weather, the last was the worst.

As it was estimated that work on repairing the bank would be completed in eight days, the opening ceremony was postponed from 5 to 13 December, but numerous other engagements prevented the Board of Trade inspector from returning until 17 December.

This time he passed the line, though recommending that the slip be watched during the winter, and that trains run cautiously. As the inspection train reached Cricklade and the other stations, bills were posted announcing that the line was passed and would be open to traffic the following day. Since Christmas was so near, Cirencester folk delayed celebrating the opening until the New Year, but Cricklade could not wait and held its jollifications in the White Hart Hotel on 21 December. Six months later, the railways south and north of Swindon were amalgamated to form the Midland & South Western Junction Railway. The line was extended to Andoversford and through trains to and from the Midland ran on 1 August 1891 (see the author's *Branch Lines of Gloucestershire*, Alan Sutton, 1991).

Two companies working trains over the single line from Savernake to Marlborough proved unsatisfactory, particularly as traffic had grown to such an extent that on average a train ran every twenty-five minutes. The MSWJR general manager, Sam Fay, found that in less than two years, one hundred and seventy MSWJR trains had been delayed by the Marlborough Railway for about half an hour, and one for no less than five hours. The travelling public was further disadvantaged by the fact that as part of the conditions for being granted running powers over the Marlborough branch, the MSWJR was not allowed to book passengers between Marlborough and Savernake and vice versa. This meant that someone wishing to travel between these two stations by an MSWJR train had to book to a station beyond; that is, from Marlborough to Grafton, or Savernake to Ogbourne, depending on the direction.

The solution was for the the MSWJR to build its own line between Marlborough and Savernake. In 1895 the Marlborough & Grafton Railway was promoted, as the MSWJR was in the Receiver's hands and could not raise the capital itself.

The new line required the 647 yd long Marlborough tunnel and so precise were the measurements that when the two headings met after five months' work, a deviation no greater than $\frac{3}{8}$ in had been made in that distance. The two and a half million bricks required for lining the tunnel came from the Malago Works, Bristol. The line's contractors, Lucas & Aird, were up-to-date and used a steam navvy to excavate cuttings. The double track line opened on 26 June 1898 and many of the MSWJR's existing single-line sections doubled during the next few years.

The MSWJR proved invaluable in the First World War carrying war supplies from the North and Midlands to the channel ports; transporting troops from the various camps in the area, and, sadly, carrying wounded soldiers from Southampton in hospital trains. Old people recalling the war still say 'Them trains never stopped' and certainly throughout the hostilities an average of 4 troop trains and 1 ambulance train ran daily. Drivers were sometimes so busy that they did not see their families for a fortnight, occasionally having to work twenty-four hours without a rest. Traffic was so heavy that additional locomotives had to be borrowed from the Great Western, London & South Western, and Midland Railways. Coaches too came from far afield, on one occasion the sidings at Ludgershall held carriages from the Great Central, Great Western, Highland, London & North Western, London & South Western, Midland, North Eastern and North British Railways.

One important commodity carried by the MSWJR was milk. Cricklade had some of the finest pasture in England and dairying was the chief farming activity. In the nineteenth century some of the milk was made into cheese, but by 1920, most milk was sent to London by rail, 12,000 gallons a day and 4 to 5 million gallons a year.

The milk trains started from Cricklade at 6.50 p.m. with four loaded vans. The guard, travelling porter (he travelled with the train and assisted loading, as the number of churns was so great that a station porter, unaided, would have taken too long) and station porter lifted the churns which weighed 2¼ cwt and held 17 gallons when full, into the vans. At Blunsdon 60 churns were loaded, 20 to 25 at Moredon, and another van was coupled on at Rushey Platt. More vans were attached at Swindon Town, some empty and some loaded. At Chiseldon at the height of the season, which was in May, 60 churns were lifted in, and another 14 were loaded at Ogbourne. At Marlborough the train picked up some more vans which had already been loaded and another one or two were added at Savernake. At Grafton 60 churns would be lifted in, this figure falling to about 40 in winter. Farmers rolled the churns to the vans, the railway staff lifting them in. It was not unknown for a porter to purposely drop a churn heavily so that milk splashed out and ran down the side making it easy for a gummed label to be attached. Between 9 and 10 p.m. the train finally arrived at Andover with seventeen loaded vans where a London & South Western engine and guard were ready to take them onwards to Clapham Junction and Waterloo.

The MSWJR crew returned from Andover at 12.15 a.m. with the empties. Dropping these off at stations was a noisy job. The churns had brass plates with the owner's name and these had to be sorted out by the light of a handlamp. Sometimes this empty milk train would stop outside Marlborough tunnel so that the crew could catch rabbits. When this happened, at the following stations the driver and fireman would come back to help with unloading to regain the lost time.

Marlborough College provided the line with worthwhile traffic. Apart from the obvious increase in passengers at the beginning and end of term, a special train being run from Marlborough to London, there were trunks, tuck boxes and bicycles, the boys being allowed an hour at lunch time to take their machines to the station. The parcel porter returning from lunch beheld a sea of bicycles, many simply dropped in a heap together causing the pedals and handlebars to interlock. Pumps fell off and as these could not be identified, they were stored in the parcels office and sold to the boys next term for a shilling each. During term time, meat and Melton Mowbray pies arrived by rail and, so that it could buy in bulk, the College owned at least three coal wagons. Nos 63, 64 and 65 were painted purple-brown with white letters shaded black. No. 64 was labelled 'Return empty to Pixton Colliery Co., Alfreton, Derbyshire'.

The MSWJR was small enough for employees to know each other, and in some ways it was like a big, happy family and certainly on some occasions life had its lighter side. Reg Hyde, an assistant guard, was very fond of practical jokes and one day, as he was passing through Marlborough tunnel, climbed on the roof of the brake van, lay flat and placed his heel on the stove pipe chimney. The guard inside experienced an unusually large quantity of smoke. He did not guess what was really happening, but missing his assistant, looked out to see if he was on the running boards. As he did this Reg, still on the roof, leaned over and touched his ear, terrifying the guard.

On another occasion in Wolfhall sidings Reg climbed on a one-plank, low-sided wagon belonging to the Bath & Portland Stone Company and, as the train climbed to Grafton, made his way over the wagons to the tender. He climbed on it, bellowed and waved his pole to frighten the driver and fireman. He certainly succeeded – the driver was leaning out of the cab and the fright made him drop his pipe over the side.

One night as a 'Down' goods hauled by a 4–4–0 was passing Ogbourne there was confusion on the footplate. The fireman believed the driver had the tablet and vice versa, but it turned out that neither had it. They stopped and went back to the signalman. He was quite adamant that he had handed it over and the footplate crew were equally sure that they had not received it. Two hours were spent looking high and low on the tracks and platforms, but all to no avail. Eventually they decided to go on without it. Strictly speaking, a pilotman should have been called out, but there were no other trains in the vicinity and the MSWJR was not a stickler for seeing that rules were obeyed. After arriving at Andover the engine was turned and someone noticed the missing tablet caught on the part of the handrail which protuded beyond the handrail support on the cabside. It was duly handed over on the return journey.

During the First World War American soldiers sometimes rode in the milk vans, some of which were old six-wheel passenger coaches still with their original passenger doors. For many years MSWJR men remembered their terror at seeing moving bodies in the darkness where no one was expected.

One day at Cricklade some white pigs were driven up to the loading dock and, very curious as pigs are, inspected a burst barrel of tar which had been brought for road repairs. They waded into it and became black. The stationmaster was very worried, expecting serious repercussions from their furious owner, but luckily there were no complaints.

During the Second World War a driver stopped at Ludgershall as an air-raid warning sounded and he could not proceed through to Andover. Having had previous experience of raids when he was narrowly missed by a fragment from a bomb at Bristol, he decided to take cover. He climbed down from the footplate and took shelter lying under one of the vans in the train. The guard came along and asked why he was lying there. The driver explained. The guard then observed that this place of refuge was not particularly safe as the van he was under contained ammunition.

The MSWJR fortunately experienced no large accident, though there were those of a more minor nature. The first fatality occurred in May 1881 when, during the SMAR's construction, a navvy tipping soil at West Grafton slipped while leading a horse drawing a loaded spoil truck and was run over by one of the wagon's wheels.

The year 1895 proved to be a relatively bad one for accidents. From Andover northwards the road had been affected by frost and all drivers were warned to 'drive carefully'. On 5 April the 9.15 a.m. passenger train from Andover became derailed at Tanner's curve almost 2½ miles north of Marlborough. The train, drawn by 2–4–0T No. 6, consisted of four six-wheelers. The engine and first two coaches went halfway down the 10 ft embankment but the other two coaches remained on the ballast. The first coach contained only two passengers, which was lucky as the tender buffers stove in one end. The other compartments were full of boys returning home for their Easter holiday. The crew were shaken, but no passengers were hurt. Lt.-Col. Yorke, the inspecting officer, considered that the warning to 'drive carefully' was inadequate.

A strange minor disaster occurred at Rushey Platt station on 26 June 1895. The lurching of the 3.10 p.m. from Andover as it passed from one curve to another near the points, caused a light four-wheel LSWR truck to become derailed shortly after passing through the loop points at the south end of the station. It was dragged along on the ballast for a quarter of a mile, striking the projecting ends of the platform's wooden joists and knocking them out of place so that the platform collapsed down the slope of the embankment. The station-master, waiting to receive the tablet, fell with the platform and was thrown down the embankment but only bruised. The signalman, further along the 150 yd platform ready to offer the tablet for the section ahead, saved himself by running down the bank at the north end of the station. The accident was caused by excessive speed.

Ogbourne was the scene of an accident on 30 April 1900. 0–6–0T No. 2 had worked the 3.15 p.m. Swindon to Ogbourne market train which consisted of two coaches and a goods brake van. On arrival at Ogbourne the engine had run round and coupled to the brake, preparatory to taking it to the other end of the train for the return journey. As the coupling chain between van and coach was tight the engine buffered up to ease it. This impact set the coaches moving. Efforts to stop them failed and they struck an 'Up' train at a good walking pace, the train itself travelling at 15 m.p.h. The engine had its chimney knocked off, the buffer beam smashed and smokebox door and brake gear damaged. One of the empty coaches had three compartments stove in. Three passengers were injured in the 'Up' train. Lt.-Col. Yorke at the Board of Trade inquiry said that the use on a passenger train of a goods brake van not fitted with a vacuum brake was contrary to a Board of Trade Order. The company explained that it was short of rolling stock and no passenger brake van was available at Swindon.

What was to prove the last mishap on the line occurred on 1 May 1964. The special bringing four hundred Marlborough College boys from Paddington arrived at Marlborough for the very last time and as the Hymek diesel was running round the train, it ran off the end of the rails. Unknown to the driver, some of the track had been lifted eight weeks previously. Six hundred gallons of fuel were spilt and railwaymen from Reading worked through the night to re-rail this, the first diesel to visit the station.

On 1 July 1923 the MSWJR was absorbed by the GWR which enabled economies to be made. For instance, the two stations at Savernake were placed under one station-master as were the two at Marlborough; the former GWR Marlborough branch was connected with the MSWJR's 'Up' line south of the tunnel so that what appeared to be double track south of Marlborough, was in fact two parallel single lines. Other significant economies were singling some of the sections and closing the MSWJR's works at Cirencester.

The first trial of the Motor Economic System of track maintenance (as opposed to just the economic system which used manually propelled vehicles), took place between Rushey Platt and Cirencester with petrol-driven trolleys in 1928. This location was chosen so that the vehicles could be conveniently monitored from Swindon.

During the Second World War the line again became a vital artery, but with the development of road transport in the 1950s it grew very uneconomic, and eventually Savernake High Level station closed on 22 June 1959. Passenger services over the whole line ceased on 11 September 1961 when much of the line was closed. Savernake Low Level to Marlborough shut on 7 September 1964, Rushey Platt to Cirencester was cut back to the electricity sidings at Moredon on 1 April 1964, this spur being closed completely in 1973. The section from Rushey Platt to Swindon Town enjoyed a brief new lease of life when it carried materials for motorway construction, but this ceased in October 1970.

At the time of writing, Hampshire and Wiltshire County Councils are investigating the possibility of re-opening the line from Andover to Ludgershall to passengers, and re-laying the track to Tidworth.

Unfortunately no MSWJR locomotive has been preserved, but 0–6–0PT No. 9400 in Swindon Museum has a boiler which was once carried by an MSWJR 4–4–4T when rebuilt by the GWR. The Swindon & Cricklade Railway Society have a centre at Blunsdon and have relaid track along the formation towards Cricklade and hope to develop further.

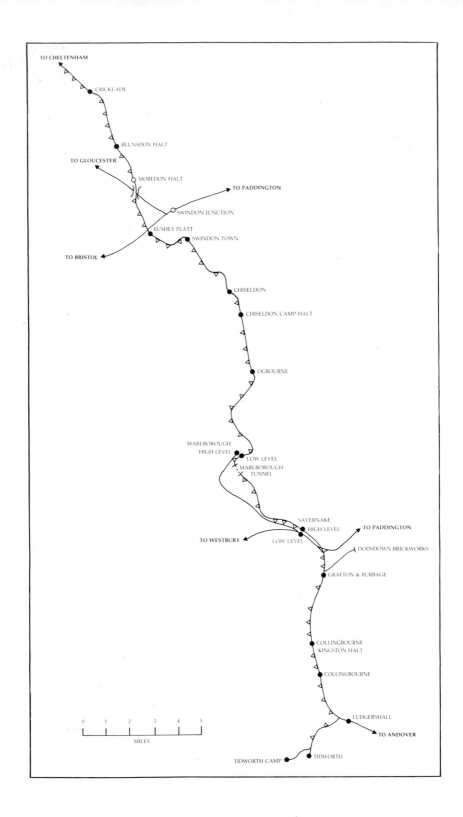

TO CHELTENHAM

CRICKLADE

BLUNSDON HALT

TO GLOUCESTER

MOREDON HALT

TO PADDINGTON

SWINDON JUNCTION

RUSHEY PLATT

SWINDON TOWN

TO BRISTOL

CHISELDON

CHISELDON CAMP HALT

OGBOURNE

MARLBOROUGH
HIGH LEVEL

LOW LEVEL
MARLBOROUGH
TUNNEL

SAVERNAKE
HIGH LEVEL

TO PADDINGTON

TO WESTBURY

LOW LEVEL

DODSDOWN BRICKWORKS

GRAFTON & BURBAGE

COLLINGBOURNE
KINGSTON HALT

COLLINGBOURNE

LUDGERSHALL

TO ANDOVER

TIDWORTH CAMP

TIDWORTH

0   1   2   3   4   5

MILES

18

Cutting the first sod of the Swindon, Marlborough & Andover Railway at Cold Harbour, Meddown, Marlborough. Within a few moments, the wheel of the ornate barrow was to break.

28.7.1875   *Illustrated London News*

Swindon, Marlborough & Andover Railway 2–4–0T No. 7 in ex-works condition. Built by Beyer, Peacock & Co. in 1882, it was withdrawn in 1910.

Author's Collection

Swindon Town, view north soon after opening. Notice the light track and sleepers covered with ballast. The company's offices were in the building above the signal-box. The waiting shelter on the 'Up' platform is similar to one on the 'Down' platform at Marlborough. This photograph shows the original run-round loop between the 'Up' and 'Down' roads. In 1905 the layout was remodelled when the 'Up' platform was made into an island and widened, only tracks then being between the platforms. At the same time, the 'Down' platform was lengthened at its northern end, resulting in a replacement signal-box having to be installed. In this view, staff and children outnumbered passengers.

c. 1881   Author's Collection

The first railway bridge across the Thames; in this view, taken near Cricklade, Gloucestershire is in the foreground and Wiltshire on the far bank.

6.5.60   Author

Swindon Town, view south. Notice that there are only two roads between the platforms. The small waiting shelter on the 'Up' platform has been replaced by a more substantial affair in brick. The locomotive is probably 0–6–0T No. 1. A goods train stands in the 'Up' loop. A 'calling-on', or repeater signal, is to the left of the footbridge.

c. 1906   Author's Collection

An MSWJR 4–4–0 heads the North Express at Swindon Town. The view was taken from the Devizes Road bridge.

c. 1914   Author's Collection

21

A. Vitti & Son's 10 ton coal wagon photographed when new at the Gloucester Railway Carriage & Wagon Co.'s works. The wagon was painted red with white lettering.

June 1904   Author's Collection

MSWJR 4–4–0 No. 8 at Marlborough with the 1.10 p.m. South Express. It is hoped that the running lad caught the train!

c. 1914   Author's Collection

The Midland and South Western Junction Station, Marlborough.

This railway forms communication towards the south with Southampton and the Isle of Wight, and on the north joins the Midland Railway at Cheltenham.

A 4-4-0 arrives at Marlborough with an 'Up' train. Behind the fence the body of a grounded vehicle acts as a store.

c. 1912   Author's Collection

Ludgershall, showing troops and horses making use of the platform, which was deliberately built wide to cope with this traffic. On the left is a line of horse boxes. The crosspiece on the signal-post is supported by an attractive bracket.

c. 1910   Lens of Sutton

2–4–0 No. 11 at Swindon Town. Built by Dübs in 1894 it lasted until withdrawn by British Railways in 1952.

Author's Collection

4–4–0 No. 9 at Swindon Town. Built by Dübs in 1893, it was withdrawn in 1924.

Author's Collection

4–4–4T No. 17 at Swindon Town. Notice the attractive monogram and lining-out. The engine was painted red, the gilt script lettering shaded blue. Notice the bottle jack on the frame above the front bogie. The headlamps had a square base and so could not be purloined by the carriage department which used a different fitting. The engine was built by Sharp Stewart in 1897 and was withdrawn in 1927.

30.4.21   Dr A.J.G. Dickens/Author's Collection

0–6–0T No. 13 at Swindon Town. Built by Dübs in 1894, it was withdrawn in 1926.

c. 1905   Author's Collection

Marlborough College 12 ton coal wagon No. 64 built by the Gloucester Carriage & Wagon Co., March 1907. It was in a livery of purple-brown with white lettering.

Author's Collection

'Cameronians' on manoeuvres at Marlborough Low Level Station. Notice the smoke from the machine guns. An 'Up' express enters, drawn by a 43xx class 2–6–0. The High Level station can be seen to the right of the signal-box.

September 1934   Author's Collection

BR No. 1336, ex-MSWJR 2–4–0 No. 12, heads a Gloucestershire Railway Society special at Swindon Town.

9.5.53 Dr A.J.G. Dickens/Author's Collection

A busy scene at Marlborough Low Level. Left, 8750 class 0–6–0PT No. 9720 heads the 2.50 p.m. Andover to Swindon Town, while SR 'U' class 2–6–0 No. 31809 arrives with the 1.52 p.m. Cheltenham to Southampton.

13.7.61 R.E. Toop

8750 class 0–6–0PT No. 9754 arrives at Marlborough Low Level with the 4.52 p.m. Swindon Town to Andover.

17.4.61   Author

The 4.52 p.m. Swindon Town to Andover departs. Milepost $19\frac{1}{2}$ is measured from Red Post Junction, Andover.

17.4.61   Author

Two fixed-distant signals south of Marlborough. At one time double track at this location, the layout was modified to two single lines. The left track came from Savernake Low Level, the right had been lifted by the time this photograph was taken.

26.2.65   Author

BR Standard class 4 2–6–0 No. 76028 leaving Collingbourne Kingston Halt with the 1.52 p.m. Cheltenham to Southampton.

17.4.61   Author

45xx class 2–6–2T No. 5555 with goods to Ludgershall, is here south of Collingbourne.
17.4.61   Author

No. 5555 having left its train in a siding, passes through Ludgershall on its way to Andover. The grass in the foreground indicates that only part of the platforms receive regular use.
17.4.61   Author

The junction at Ludgershall showing the Tidworth branch curving left, and the main line to Swindon, right. Towards the skyline is Windmill Camp. The Midland Railway wagons on the left probably contain bricks for constructing Tidworth Barracks. Towards the centre of the picture is the engine shed, with a corrugated-iron goods shed further to the right. On the left, post and rail fencing changes to post and wire, the latter being a more common MSWJR boundary.

c. 1905   Author's Collection

King George V at Ludgershall after inspecting troops. The London & North Western Railway Royal Train is at the platform. Coincidentally a LNWR notice-board faces the camera.

8.11.17   Author's Collection

31

E. Neale, head permanent way ganger at Cirencester, on a new motor trolley tested on the MSWJR. The petrol-driven engine is beneath his seat. Handles are provided for lifting the trolley off the running track when the workmen reached the length needing attention. This photograph was made into a cigarette card by Messrs W.D. & H.O. Wills.

c. 1934   Author's Collection

A more modern permanent way motor ganger trolley and trailer on the 'Up' line at Marlborough Low Level. Side sheets were provided to keep out the rain, wind, or sun.

13.7.61   R.E. Toop

Hymek diesel-hydraulic D7044 with a goods train on a misty spring morning, standing at the 'Down' platform, Swindon Town. Although no passenger trains have run for 3½ years, the station is in good condition.

29.4.65   Author

A dramatic pile-up at Swindon Town. Boys had released the wagons' brakes and the trucks ran off the end of the siding.

14.9.70   Author's Collection

This photograph was taken from almost the same viewpoint as the illustration on p. 31 when BR Standard class 4 2–6–4T No. 80065 was shunting at Ludgershall. The branch to the War Department lines is on the left, with trap points to divert runaways before they fouled the running line; the goods shed is centre. Straight ahead is the former main line to Swindon, the track of which is lifted beyond the overbridge.

1965   Paul Strong

BR Standard class 4 2–6–4T No. 80065 leaving Ludgershall for Andover.

1965   Paul Strong

Army locomotive No. 8219 at Ludgershall coupled to two ex-SR goods brake vans.

29.4.65   Author

Blunsdon station on the Swindon & Cricklade Railway. A Fowler locomotive works No. 4210137 stands at the rebuilt platform. The bricks forming the path in the foreground came from Swindon Town station.

15.5.89   Author

Swindon & Cricklade Railway: the view north from Blunsdon from the cab of a Fowler locomotive works No. 4210137.

15.5.89   Author

Dodsdown Brickworks Railway

Around the turn of the century the Army required large quantities of bricks to develop Salisbury Plain as a military training ground with depots at places such as Tidworth, Bulford and Larkhill. Clay suitable for brickmaking was not common in Wiltshire, so building materials were brought from all over the country for the vast barracks at Tidworth. In 1902 clay was found 8 miles from Tidworth, at Dodsdown, 2 miles north-east of the MSWJR's Grafton station. The contractor, A.J. Keeble of Peterborough, built a 2 mile long standard gauge line from Dodsdown Brickworks to Grafton. The layout at Dodsdown was simple, just consisting of three sidings serving dryers, kilns, boiler house and engine shed.

The locomotive used for the construction of the line and the first services was *A.J. Keeble*, an 0–6–0ST built by Peckett & Sons of Bristol in 1902 as works No. 939. As the gradient rose from Grafton to Dodsdown, normal practice was to push the wagons in this direction and haul them in the other, a wise precaution in days when wagon couplings were made of inferior steel. On several occasions, particularly in damp weather, *A.J. Keeble* lost its grip and the complete train slid back down the gradient. In 1907 it was transferred to the Wissington Light Railway, Norfolk, and replaced by an 0–4–0ST Peckett, works No. 1080, named *Progress*. Braking was by handbrake only, surprising after the experience with the early engine, and hazardous on those gradients. *A.J. Keeble* had been painted Midland lake and black with a brass dome, but *Progress* sported a livery of apple green. Both engines were owned by Keeble and officially used exclusively on his private line, but in practice the staff at Grafton station was not above coming to terms with the driver of *Progress* when a van or two needed moving in the MSWJR yard.

To keep the builders supplied and the brickworks provided with fuel, trains ran as necessary, usually two journeys being made in each direction daily. The load was normally six wagons: four empty brick wagons and two loaded coal wagons from Grafton to Dodsdown, and four loaded brick and two empty coal wagons from Dodsdown to Grafton.

It was the practice for the fireman to open the gates at Heath Lane level crossing and close them after the train had passed. The width of the track bed was less than that of the road, so the gates were fitted with hinged extensions which had to be opened out when the gates were across the thoroughfare. Local boys, knowing when a train was due, would sometimes have the gates already open, and after closing them would get their reward, a ride to Grafton, either on the footplate or on the bricks. One one occasion, the driver released his handbrake a little early and the train came hurtling down the 1 in 60 gradient without any hope of stopping at the level crossing – but the lads were there, the gates open and *Progress* sped a further half mile to Grafton station before she could be stopped. The local boys were also useful for gathering bracken and long grass to clean out the brick dust and straw from the wagons.

Another incident, which happily did not end in disaster, occurred when, while shunting at Dodsdown, two wagons whose brakes were not securely pinned, ran down the gradient through the three sets of double gates and three single gates between fields.

The Tidworth barracks were completed by 1910 and the line closed and dismantled shortly afterwards. *Progress* was sent to Sanderson Bros & Newbould Ltd, Sheffield.

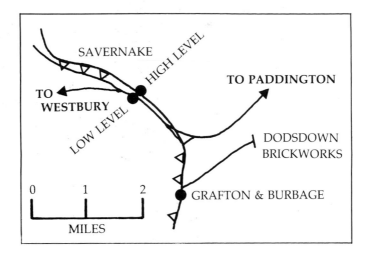

A.J. Keeble, a Peckett 0–6–0ST belonging to the Dodsdown Brickworks line, on the main MSWJR 'Down' line at Marlborough, perhaps being delivered when new, or returning after repair.

Author's Collection

Ludgershall to Tidworth

When James Purkess, the MSWJR's new general manager learned about the military camp being erected at Tidworth, he arranged with the War Department for a railway to be built to it from his company's line at Ludgershall. Constructed on WD land, it opened for military manoeuvre traffic on 8 July 1901. At first for WD use only, public goods were carried from 1 July 1902 and public passengers from 1 October the same year. Although the track was double to Perham signal-box half a mile from Ludgershall, usually this box was switched out and the branch worked as single throughout.

Henry Lovatt, the contractor responsible for building the camp, in return for a yearly toll was allowed by the MSWJR to convey his workmen for their huts at Brimstone Bottom (nicknamed 'Tin Town') to Tidworth by his own engines, vehicles and staff.

The branch certainly justified its existence. In 1922 the garrison accommodated about 8,000 troops, while up to 100,000 were accommodated in summer camps in the surrounding district. The seven sidings in the yard held 290 wagons, or 10 trains of 12 coaches each. Days when the Tidworth Tattoo were held were particularly hectic, trains arriving from the GWR, SR and LMS systems and having to be stabled most carefully to enable them to leave in the correct order. Receipts at Tidworth, the only MSWJR station lit by electricity, were the greatest on the system, while the station was in charge of the railway's highest-ranking station-master. A curiosity was that when buying a ticket at Tidworth, the passenger stood in Hampshire and the booking clerk in Wiltshire.

The only train run on Sundays on the Tidworth branch was from Ludgershall to Tidworth for the benefit of servicemen returning from leave. The front portion of the Andover to Swindon train worked this, the remainder being left standing at Ludgershall until the engine returned from Tidworth to take it forward. In winter, vociferous complaints were often made that the Swindon portion grew very cold while waiting for 30 minutes. Public services were withdrawn on 19 September 1953 and closure was made complete beyond Perham Down on 31 July 1963, though the one third of a mile remnant still remains open for Ministry of Defence traffic. Until 1953 Tidworth Camp, across the border in Hampshire, was served by an extensive rail system owned and worked by WD locomotives.

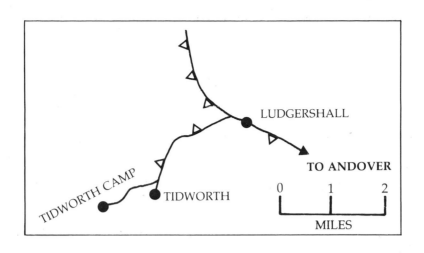

LUDGERSHALL

TO ANDOVER

TIDWORTH CAMP

TIDWORTH

0   1   2

MILES

Tidworth station with a four-coach train. Note the shine on the buffers of the tank engine. The engine shed, whose roof can just be seen to the right of the last coach, was removed to another position in 1915 to make room for increased siding accommodation.

c. 1913   Paul Strong Collection

41

The four-coach branch set at Tidworth standing clear of the run-round loop. The goods shed can be seen to the left of the first coach.

c. 1913   Lens of Sutton

GWR 0–6–0PT hauling a military train has drawn up at the troop platform.

c. 1932   Lens of Sutton

43xx class 2–6–0 No. 5396 has arrived at Tidworth with the afternoon train from Ludgershall. The B-set comprised coaches W6898W and W6899W, both built in 1934.

7.9.55   Hugh Ballantyne

Savernake to Marlborough

Until the completion of the GWR in 1841, Marlborough prospered by being on the coach road between Bristol, Bath and London, but then the railway which had captured all the passenger traffic passed through Swindon instead of Marlborough. The opening of Marlborough College in 1843 helped employment in the area and within thirty years became so popular that the number of pupils had grown to five hundred. At the end of each term, many boys walked to the railway at Swindon 12 miles distant, or Hungerford 11 miles away. Their boxes and their less active fellow pupils travelled by vehicle. Because of the transport problems, the school had a two term year, three terms only being introduced in 1873 following the advent of the railway.

It was not surprising that the leading proponent of the Marlborough Railway project was the Revd J.S. Thomas, Bursar of Marlborough College. The line was to branch from the Berks. & Hants. Extension Railway at Savernake.

An Act was obtained in 1861 and with Lord Bruce as chairman of the railway company, shares were readily subscribed for, but then, curiously, no action was taken until the contractor, John Knight of Newbury, started work in the spring of 1863 without any ceremony of cutting the first turf. Work proceeded rapidly and on 8 March 1864 Captain Rich arrived to inspect the line. Although most items gained his approval, he found that one embankment was not sufficiently consolidated and stop blocks were required at all the sidings, so he did not grant a certificate. Matters corrected, Captain Rich paid a return visit on 30 March when he had quite an exciting time. The engine supplied by the GWR stalled many times on the gradients of 1 in 58–60 and rumour has it that passengers got out and pushed. This led to humorous postcards being sold in Marlborough with the train depicted as the Marlborough Donkey and the caption:

> 'You may push and you may shuv
> But I'm hanged if I'll be druv'.

The Marquess of Ailesbury's comment at the post-inspection luncheon that the line would appear in *Bradshaw* in a few days, led a man to come from Avebury to travel on it and find to his chagrin that traffic would not begin until after the meeting with the Great Western Board. The Marlborough Railway was opened on 14 April 1864 and a horse bus connected it with Calne. In October the directors discussed extending the line as far as Calne, but decided against the idea.

The line was converted to standard gauge on 27 June 1874, reopening on 1 July; the Berks. & Hants. Extension Railway being altered at the same time. The GWR informed the Marlborough Railway that the estimated cost of the conversion would be £2,600 and that it would lend the money. The Marlborough Railway replied that it had no funds and its borrowing powers were completely taken up; even an interest of 5 per cent on the cost would render an ordinary dividend only an irregular occurence. Later it was amicably arranged that the Marlborough Railway would only pay half the cost of conversion, not exceeding £750, at a rate of 4 per cent interest. The GWR accountants seem to have been pleasantly slow, not working out the expense of narrowing the gauge until 1877 and fortunately only charging the Marlborough Railway £296 11s. 8d.

Savernake station was interesting for the fact that it was built above the Kennet & Avon Canal tunnel. At Marlborough, as occurred on quite a number of branch lines, the engine shed water tank was filled by a steam pump powered by the branch engine. The whistle was unscrewed, a pipe connected, the whistle chain secured down and the water raised from well to tank. This operation had to be carried out about twice weekly.

As was recounted on p. 12, the Marlborough Railway gave running powers to the Swindon, Marlborough & Andover Railway and its successor the Midland & South Western Junction Railway, until the Marlborough & Grafton Railway was opened, when traffic became less hectic. On 6 March 1933 the GWR's engineers south of Marlborough tunnel diverted the Marlborough Railway into the former MSWJR's 'Up' line, thus saving maintenance on about 2½ miles of track. Marlborough High Level was closed to passengers on this date, but a connection with the Low Level line still made it accessible to goods trains.

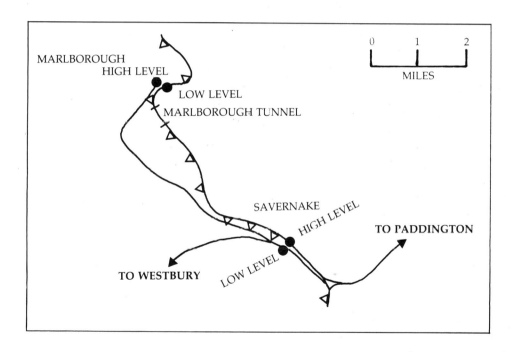

An 0–6–0PT heads a train for Swindon Town standing in the bay platform at Savernake Low Level. The west end of the Kennet & Avon Canal tunnel is immediately to the right of Savernake West signal-box. Notice the junction signals on the left which are smaller than usual. The bare earth of the cutting of the MSWJR line serving Savernake High Level station can be seen to the left of the nearest telegraph pole.

c. 1960   Lens of Sutton

A 'Metro' class 2–4–0T leaves Savernake Low Level for Marlborough High Level. The two coaches are ex-MSWJR stock repainted in the GWR chocolate and cream livery. Notice the water tank set into the cutting.

1928   Lens of Sutton

Platform at Marlborough High Level, with the former locomotive shed which ceased to be used for this purpose in March 1933. Below the loading gauge can be seen Marlborough Low Level station and signal-box.

17.4.61   Author

GWR Milnes Daimler 20 hp double-decker bus AF 64 at Marlborough High Level station working the service to Calne. To the left of the entrance a board reads 'Marlborough – Calne'. The siphon van between the station building and signal-box probably contained milk churns.

c. 1909   GWR

Dauntsey to Malmesbury

The Malmesbury branch was unique in the fact that it changed its junction from one main line to another of equal importance.

One of the first railway schemes to mention Malmesbury was the Wiltshire & Gloucestershire Railway authorized by Parliament in 1864. The GWR and the Midland Railway were at loggerheads at the time and this line was an attempt by the directors of the Midland to make an inroad into their rival's territory. The Midland agreed to work the line as a continuation of its Stonehouse & Nailsworth Railway. It was to run from Nailsworth, through Tetbury and Malmesbury to Christian Malford on the main GWR line to Bristol. Needless to say, it was not the village of Christian Malford which was the ultimate objective, but Salisbury and the south coast. The following year, powers were obtained for a North & South Wiltshire Junction Railway to run from Christian Malford to the Berks. & Hants. Extension Railway between Woodborough and Devizes, while the Wiltshire Railway was to carry it on to Salisbury.

Even though the Wiltshire & Gloucestershire Railway was authorized by Parliament, the Midland's little scheme did not materialize. It so happened that in a previous dispute between the GWR and the MR over inroads into each other's territory, an agreement was made that they should 'agree as to subscribing to any new lines in the districts in which the companies are directly interested'. Captain Galton of the Board of Trade was appointed arbitrator to decide if this new scheme contravened the agreement. Deciding that it did, he had the local companies dissolved in 1870. It is known that work was actually started on the Wiltshire & Gloucestershire Railway at Malmesbury in July 1865, possibly on the tunnel, but so far no evidence has come to light. The work was abandoned after the arbitrator's decision had been made known.

Malmesbury was still determined to have a railway and met with success in July 1872 when the Malmesbury Railway received its Act. The line was to run from GWR at Dauntsey to Malmesbury, a distance of 6½ miles, the GWR agreeing to subscribe half the estimated cost of £60,000 and work the line on completion.

The first sod was cut on 8 July 1874. The line was completed and on 17 December 1877 opened 'amid much rejoicings'. Free tickets were issued to shareholders who travelled by special train to Malmesbury and were received by a procession of leading inhabitants. Regular traffic started the next day when a mishap occurred. The *Swindon Advertiser* of 22 December reports:

Accident on the Malmesbury and Dauntsey Railway – An accident happened on Tuesday on the new line of railway, that was opened on the previous day from Malmesbury to Dauntsey Station, but happily did not result in any material damage to life or property. The accident in question took place at the [Dauntsey Road] level crossing between Dauntsey and Somerford Magna, [Great Somerford] where there was a pair of 'massive gates' erected across the railway, and also a gate-keeper's

48

house. As the early train was proceeding from Dauntsey, the gate-keeper failed to open the gates, and the train dashed through, shivering the gate to atoms. Beyond slight damage to the engine, no further damage was done. From inquiries it appears that the old man at the gates could not get out of the house in time owing to the handle of the door coming off in his hand. He had been in the service of the company for 35 years, and this is the first accident he has ever had. There will be an inquiry into the matter.

Just over two years later, a more serious tragedy was averted. As a consequence of heavy rain during the morning of 3 March, Swallett's Brook rose rapidly, the strong current washing away the foundation of a pier at Poole's Bridge between Dauntsey and Somerford. The 11.35 a.m. from Dauntsey safely crossed this bridge, but shortly afterwards the buttress on the left bank collapsed, shifting the 53 ft span by several feet. Fortunately two sixteen-year-old boys foresaw the danger and alerted the train to it, which was due to return as the 12 o'clock from Malmesbury. The *Bath & Cheltenham Chronicle* recorded that:

> They ran with all speed and by extended arms and the waving of their hands, succeeded in attracting the attention of the policeman [i.e. gate keeper] at the crossing and he stopped the train which had just appeared in sight. The train proceeded slowly on until it met the lads and they informed the driver of the state of the bridge. The train was backed to Somerford where the passengers, numbering less than a dozen, got out and proceeded to walk to Dauntsey, a distance of about three miles.

For the rest of the day, the GWR provided a horse-drawn conveyance between Dauntsey and Somerford. The following day a crane lifted the bridge which was then fixed temporarily so that passengers could detrain on one side, walk across and entrain beyond. The bridge was re-opened for rail traffic on 9 March. The Malmesbury Railway was taken over by the GWR from 1 July 1892.

The Bristol & South Wales Direct Railway, a shorter route from Wootton Bassett to the Severn tunnel than that via Bristol, opened in 1903. When this line was under construction, a temporary connection was laid from the Malmesbury branch westwards for the purpose of bringing materials to the new line. Some thirty years later, as an economy measure, it was decided that a permanent connection line would be laid alongside the relatively new 'Up' Badminton line from Little Somerford station to the Malmesbury branch at Kingsmead crossing. These alterations were completed by 6 February 1933 so that the branch could be worked from Little Somerford instead of Dauntsey, but a legal hitch prevented the abandonment from Kingsmead crossing to Dauntsey. The new spur was not used until 17 July when the line between Dauntsey and Kingsmead crossing was closed. The length of the branch was now 3¾ instead of 6½ miles.

The original Malmesbury Railway used a short terminal bay platform at the west end of the 'Up' platform at Dauntsey and this remained in situ until dismantled in April 1956, the platform canopy seeing further service sheltering Clevedon trains at Yatton. Immediately south of Great Somerford station a lane was crossed by the railway, the bridge leaving a headroom of only 7 ft. Clearly this was insufficient for many vehicles, so the railway built a parallel road with a level crossing, this being given over to the Wiltshire County Council when the line was abandoned. The station building and platform at Great Somerford were constructed of timber and sold for £10 when this section of the line closed. A single-storey cottage was provided for the crossing keeper. The heavy milk traffic which developed (sometimes as many as 100 cartloads of churns came from farms daily), made it necessary for a station-master to be appointed. He had a large family and needed a bigger house, so this was arranged by the simple expedient of adding an upper storey in 1893 at a cost of £127. With the opening of the main-line station at Little Somerford, traffic fell and Great Somerford became a halt – milk consignment notes being collected by the gatekeeper, while passenger tickets were issued and collected by the guard.

The rails between Dauntsey and Great Somerford were lifted soon after the branch was curtailed, but a short spur between Great Somerford and Kingsmead crossing remained for stabling wagons awaiting repair, and during the Second World War for storing restaurant cars, these having been withdrawn in order to give more passenger accommodation. When this track was lifted in March 1959, wagons sent to pick up the old rails came off the end of the line and knocked a hole in the former station house.

North of Great Somerford the line passed under the Bristol & South Wales Direct Railway and came to Kingsmead crossing where the new branch from Little Somerford joined the former Kingsmead siding which was the truncated old branch. Little Somerford on the South Wales line was quite a large station. It had four tracks, the two in the centre being used by through trains, while those serving the platforms were used by stopping trains, or goods trains waiting to be overtaken by expresses. Malmesbury services could leave from either platform.

Just before entering Malmesbury station, the branch line ran through a 105 yd long tunnel. The situation of the station was rather unusual in that it lay beyond the town, rather than short of it, as was the case with so many branches. Possibly this was the result of the abortive Wiltshire & Gloucestershire Railway project.

In the days when the branch ran from Dauntsey to Malmesbury, seven trains ran each way daily taking between sixteen and twenty-three minutes for the journey. Several of them were 'mixed'. In 1933 when trains commenced running to and from Little Somerford, nine trips were run each way and nine minutes were allowed for the journey. The branch train made an evening trip to Swindon and back, and an afternoon trip to and from Wootton Bassett, an additional train running mornings from Swindon to Malmesbury. Except for the 'mixed' trips, there were no guards on the branch trains.

On Sunday 2 October 1927, No. 13, a Sentinel geared locomotive was tried over the branch with a view to reducing the operating costs. The engine made a satisfactory run with a passenger train reaching a maximum speed of 38 m.p.h., but a 'mixed' train of normal formation proved to be beyond its capacity. This engine had a patent, geared chain-drive, steam being produced in a vertical, instead of horizontal, boiler. Its appearance was curious as everything, including the boiler, was within the large cab – only the coal bunker was outside. Until its withdrawal in 1946, it spent most of its time shunting in the Park Royal Trading Estate.

Thirteen coach trains were the longest that could be dealt with at Malmesbury, Sunday School specials often being of this length. One evening in June 1940, a thirteen coach train full of evacuees arrived at Malmesbury behind two tender engines. A marquee had been set up in the station forecourt and here food was issued to the evacuees before they were marched to Malmesbury Grammar School for a medical inspection and taken to their billets.

With increasing competition from road transport in post-war years, passenger services were no longer economic and the last ran on 8 September 1951. The still substantial goods traffic continued. Inwards chiefly consisting of coal, cattle feed, paper, components for the Ekco radio factory, and farm machinery for repair by A.B. Blanch. Outwards traffic was principally Blanch agricultural machinery, sometimes a train load of thirty wagons being despatched. About 1959 the 0–4–2T working the branch was replaced by an 03 class 0–6–0 diesel, unpopular with main line signalmen as their slow speed between Swindon and Little Somerford caused them to occupy sections for an inordinate length of time. The reason given by BR for closure on 11 November 1962 was collapsing culverts. Track was lifted the following year.

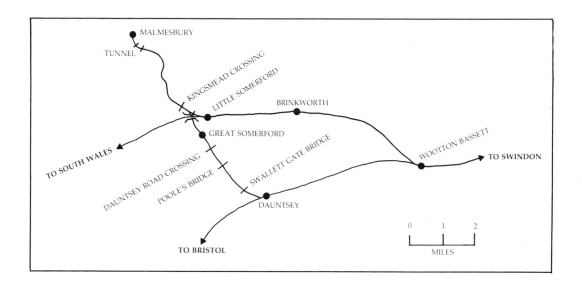

Coffee Pot, the vertical-boilered contractor's engine and wagon engaged in building the Malmes-bury branch.

1876   Author's Collection

A poster advertising a flower show at Great Somer-ford, 22 August 1907.

Author's Collection

Great Somerford station view towards Malmesbury. Notice that both the station and platform are constructed of timber and the flat-bottomed rails are spiked directly to the sleepers. The station had only five months' use before closure. Behind the bay window was the signal-box. This controlled the goods siding which was closed 22 May 1922. The building cost £200 in 1877.

February 1933   Lens of Sutton

The line from Great Somerford to Kingsmead crossing was retained after 1933 for stabling purposes. This view looks northwards from Great Somerford.

23.8.55   Author

FARINGDON BRANCH.

SINGLE LINE worked by Train Staff, assisted with 1 ock Telegraph. Form of Staff and Ticket, Triangular: Colour, Varnished Oak.

DOWN TRAINS.

Distance M.C.	STATIONS	Station No.	Ruling gradient 1 in	Point to Point times Mins.	Allow for stop Mins.	Allow for start Mins.	1 Mixed A.M.	2 Mixed A.M.	3 Mixed A.M.	4 Pass. A.M.	5 Pass. P.M.	6 Pass. P.M.
	Uffington .. dep.	136	—			1	7 22	8 36	10 30	11 22	12 15	1 18
3 41	Faringdon .... arr.	168	86 R	10	1		7 31	8 45	10 39	11 29	12 22	1 25

WEEK DAYS.—continued. / **SUNDAYS.**

STATIONS	7 Mixed	8 Pass.	9 Pass.	10 Pass.	11 Mixed	12	13	1	2	3 G Eng.& Van. N	4
	P.M.	P.M.	P.M.	P.M.	P.M.					P.M.	
Uffington .. .. dep.	2 43	4 13	7 5	7 55	8 55	..	..	..	..	6 5	..
Faringdon .... arr.	2 52	4 20	7 12	8 2	9 4	....	....	..	..	6 14	....

UP TRAINS.

STATIONS	Ruling gradient 1 in	Point to point times Mins.	Allow for stop Mins.	Allow for start Mins.	1 Pass. A.M.	2 Pass. A.M.	3 Mixed A.M.	4 Pass. A.M.	5 Pass. A.M.	6 Mixed P.M.	7 Pass. P.M.	8 Mixed P.M.
Faringdon .. dep.	—			1	6 55	7 55	10 0	11 5	11 55	12 55	2 15	3 45
Uffington .... arr.	86 F	9	1		7 2	8 2	10 9	11 12	12 2	1 4	2 22	3 54

WEEK DAYS / **SUNDAYS.**

STATIONS	9 Mixed	10 Pass.	11 Pass.	12	13	14	15	16	1	2	3C Milk and Cattle N
	P.M.	P.M.	P.M.								P.M.
Faringdon .. dep.	6 10	7 40	8 35	..	..	..	..	..	..	..	6 30
Uffington .... arr.	6 17	7 47	8 42	....	....	..	..	..	..	..	6 39

J On the first Tuesday of each month the Faringdon Branch engine and guard after arrival at Faringdon at 10.34 a.m. will return to Uffington to fetch cattle wagons. The cattle traffic will be worked to Uffington by the Special ex Faringdon and either the 2.35 p.m. ex Southall or 6.10 p.m. ex Reading may be stopped at Uffington to pick up cattle for Swindon and beyond.

Such wagons must be placed ready to be picked up at one shunt.

Uffington to ascertain from Didcot the running of these trains and advise latter point which train will be required to call for the cattle traffic.

N This trip is worked by engine and men of 5.0 p.m. Goods ex Swindon.

MALMESBURY BRANCH.

Single Line, worked by Train Staff, and only one Engine in Steam at a time (or two or more coupled). The Engineers have absolute occupation of the Malmesbury Branch each morning from 5.0 a.m. until the first train is due to leave Malmesbury. See Appendix.

DOWN TRAINS.

Distances M.C.	STATIONS	Ruling gradient 1 in	Station No.	1 Mixed A.M.	2 Mixed on last Wednesday in each month Z	3 Mixed A.M.	4 Pass. A.M.	5 Pass. Z P.M.	6 Mixed P.M.	7 Pass. P.M.	8 Pass. P.M.	Sun. 1 Pass. P.M.
—	Dauntsey .. dep.	....	1035	8 20		10 20	11 38	1 25	3 30	6 15	8 0	7 45
2 53	Great Somerford ,,	94 F	1148	8 26		10 26	11 44	1 31	3 41	6 21	8 8	7 51
6 45	Malmesbury arr.	116 R	1149	8 38		10 36	11 54	1 41	3 53	6 31	8 18	8 3

UP TRAINS.

STATIONS	Ruling gradient 1 in	1 Pass. A.M.	2 Pass. A.M.	3 Pass. A.M.	4	5 Mixed P.M.	6	7 Pass. Z P.M.	8 Mixed P.M.	9 Pass. D P.M.	10	Sun. 1 Pass.
Malmesbury dep.	....	7 13	9 18	11 3	..	12 5	..	2 6	4 53	7 2	..	5 22
Great Somerford ,,	116 F	7 23	9 28	11 13	....	12 15	....	2 16	5 4	7 18	....	5 32
Dauntsey arr.	94 R	7 29	9 34	11 19	..	12 21	..	2 22	5 11	7 25	..	5 45

D To convey passengers, also milk for London Stations, to go forward from Dauntsey by ... Chippenham Milk train.

Malmesbury branch working timetable 13 July to 20 September 1925.

The former Malmesbury bay at Dauntsey. This platform canopy was eventually moved to cover the Clevedon bay at Yatton. The Malmesbury branch curved to the right of the signal-box.

23.8.55   Author

58xx class 0–4–2T No. 5802 with goods from Malmesbury, north of Kingsmead crossing.

23.8.55   Author

A one-coach train at Malmesbury. The platform is wider than at many branch terminii and the stone station and its chimney is most attractive. The corrugated-iron hut in the lower left-hand corner is the lamp hut containing a 40 gallon drum of paraffin and spare signal lamps. On the left is the engine shed, and between it and the locomotive is a gas cylinder wagon for recharging the coach's lighting system. Beyond the passenger station is the stone-built goods shed. This view is from the buffer stops. The card was postmarked 14 January 1905.

Paul Strong Collection

58xx class 0–4–2T No. 5800 at Malmesbury with a passenger train to Little Somerford. The brake van on the right is labelled 'Malmesbury RU', the 'RU' standing for 'Restricted Use'.

10.7.50 Lens of Sutton

58xx class 0–4–2T No. 5802 at Malmesbury with an enthusiasts' special trip.
18.8.57 Trevor J. Saunders

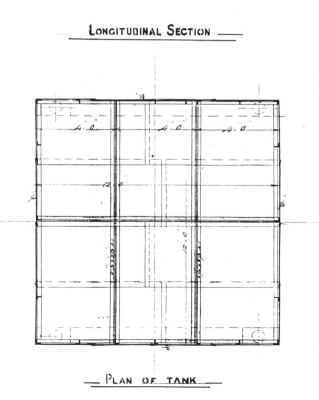

LONGITUDINAL SECTION

PLAN OF TANK

Plan of the Malmesbury water tank.

D.J. Hyde Collection

Malmesbury locomotive shed with 58xx class 0–4–2T No. 5802 standing beyond. The coal stage is centre right, with the 5,850 gallon water tank above. The timber building on the far right is the pump house, the pump being operated by steam supplied by a locomotive.

18.8.57   Trevor J. Saunders

58xx class 0–4–2T No. 5802 at Malmesbury shed. Notice the shunter's pole resting on the coupling hook and buffer.

23.8.55   Author

No. 5802 shunting at Malmesbury. This view looks towards the buffers. The track in the foreground is on wartime 'pot-type' sleepers, held to gauge at intervals by bars. This was an attempt to overcome a shortage of timber.

23.8.55   Author

View towards the terminus from Malmesbury tunnel. The fixed-distant signal shows in this view.

23.8.55   Author

D2187 shunting the daily pick-up goods at Malmesbury. Notice the hay-making machinery on the platform waiting to be loaded onto wagons. The windows of the passenger station building have been boarded up and the track to the engine shed lifted.

12.6.62   Hugh Ballantyne

D2187 arrives at Malmesbury. Centre left, farm machinery on wagons awaits collection, and more on the passenger platform is ready for loading.

15.6.62   Author

D2187 arrives at Malmesbury from Little Somerford. The goods shed is on the far left.

15.6.62   Author

Chippenham to Calne

Following the opening of the GWR, stage coaches ceased to run along the London Road through Calne, thus placing the town in something of a backwater. Calne's inhabitants realized that trade would improve if a railway was opened to the town. There was certainly sufficient traffic to warrant a line being built, as sixteen mills were within a three mile radius, not to mention the largest bacon business in England.

November 1859 saw a meeting called in the Town Hall when it appeared that the sole opponent of the scheme was the owner of a wharf on the Calne arm of the Wilts. & Berks. Canal. The necessary Act was passed in 1860 and the first sod turned in a field at Studley on 25 June 1861. A year later the contractor, Richard Hattersley of Nursling, Southampton, had made excellent progress, not being delayed by poor weather. Although everything seemed to be going well, there was trouble lurking beneath the surface. In June 1863 it was revealed that expenses had been underestimated to the tune of £10,000. Furthermore the GWR, which was to work the line, had discovered that the permanent way was shoddily constructed. Eventually matters were corrected and the Board of Trade inspecting officer Captain H.W. Tyler visited the line and passed it fit for public passenger traffic.

The Calne Railway opened for freight traffic on 29 October 1863, the first train arriving at 8.30 a.m. laden with about one hundred pigs and other goods. The opening to passengers came on 3 November. The shops were closed and a holiday was declared at Calne. The band of the 4th Wilts. Volunteer Corps in uniform paraded through the principal streets and at 10 a.m. was met by 60 employees of Messrs G. & C. Harris's bacon factory, whom they escorted to the railway station where a large number of people waited for the excursion to Bath which was to form the inaugural train. About 800 boarded it, but many more were left behind through lack of accommodation. All the employees of Messrs Harris, together with railwaymen at Calne, were treated by the firm to a 'sumptuous repast', Harris's also paying employees' excursion fares to Bath. The Calne Railway directors gave a dinner at the White Hart Hotel for 60 guests. At first five trains were run each way, but this number had risen to seventeen ninety-eight years later.

During the first month of operation the line was used by 3,918 passengers, 1,781 cattle – probably chiefly pigs – and $788\frac{1}{4}$ tons of goods. Unfortunately the company's debts were so great that they proved impossible to pay, the only solution being to sell the line to the GWR. This was done on 1 July 1892.

Perhaps the grandest day for the Calne branch was 22 July 1907 when King Edward VII and Queen Alexandra, having spent the weekend with the Marquess of Lansdowne at Bowood, returned from Calne to Paddington. By 10 a.m. all the milk churns had been removed from the passenger platform at Calne and after 10.45 the public was excluded. The station was decorated with flags and bunting, the booking office floor was carpeted for the occasion and floral arrangements were in evidence. The royal train left Calne at

11.15 a.m. and arrived at Chippenham thirteen minutes later, the branch engine being detached from one end and the engine for London attached at the other.

Fortunately no serious accident ever occurred on the branch, mishaps being relatively minor, although one of these was quite spectacular. On 18 May 1955 a shunter placed cattle trucks in the pig siding at Calne and seemingly failed to re-set the points for the loop. When the goods train arrived, its driver seeing the road incorrectly set, applied his brakes more firmly, but the wheels locked. The train continued, striking the cattle wagons and causing £7,000 worth of damage, although the only harm incurred by the engine was two broken bricks in the firebox arch.

Around the turn of the century it was proposed to extend the Calne branch to Marlborough and link with the MSWJR's Swindon to Andover line. The idea was modified to a far cheaper option of a railway bus service from Calne to Marlborough. Starting on 10 October 1904, it was one of the earliest motor bus services in the county. Three trips were run each way daily taking an hour and twenty-five minutes each way for the distance of 12¾ miles. The Milnes Daimler bus seated ten passengers inside, plus two outside beside the driver, while between the driver's back and the passenger section was a compartment for luggage, mail or goods, or by means of flap seats, passengers wishing to smoke. This latter compartment seated eight passengers.

An interesting feature of the steam trains on the branch was that to avoid the engine having to run round its train at Calne or Chippenham, many were auto worked. This meant that on arrival at Calne the engine stayed at the same end, the driver walking down the train to a control compartment at its tail, the fireman remaining on the engine at what was now the rear. The auto train replaced the steam railmotor, which was a coach with boiler and power unit on the same underframe and a driving compartment provided at each end. Although useful for ordinary traffic, the railmotor had not the power of a separate engine and this meant that when extra traffic needed to be carried, it was not strong enough to pull more than one extra coach, or a few vans of pigs.

The Calne branch was very unusual for a short line in that it was worked by engines from no less than four sheds – Chippenham, Westbury, Bath and Bristol.

Officially speed on the branch was restricted to a maximum of 30 m.p.h., though one Bath engine reached Chippenham signal-box in 7½ minutes, making an average speed of about 43 m.p.h.

On Saturday evenings during the Second World War there were usually many servicemen on the last train and it was common practice for it not to stop at Black Dog Halt on the 'Down' journey. This was because members of the armed forces the worse for drink would alight thinking it was Calne and the guard would experience difficulty getting them on board again. To avoid this problem, it was the custom to tell local residents who wanted to get off at Black Dog, that they would be carried through to Calne and dropped off on the return to Chippenham. On any train a guard always had be be on the lookout for unsuspecting servicemen getting off at Black Dog. The trouble arose because Black Dog, being a private station, did not appear in the timetable and Stanley Bridge Halt was the only published intermediate stop. Strangers therefore naturally thought that the stop after Stanley Bridge must be Calne.

Black Dog was opened in 1875 as a private station for the Marquess of Lansdowne, though the public was allowed to use it. The Marquess paid part of the station-master's wages and provided him with a house and four tons of coal annually. It did not become a public station until 15 September 1952, its first nameboard being erected just before Christmas. Until that year the halt did not exist for ticket purposes, passengers booking

63

5 November 1875. A standard-gauge goods which had left Salisbury at 3.15 p.m., ignored the danger signals as it approached Thingley Junction and proceeded towards the main line. The driver of the approaching 2.30 p.m. Paddington to Bristol broad-gauge express saw what was happening, sounded his brake whistle and reversed his engine. (At this period passenger coaches wre not fitted with continuous brakes operated from the engine, but guards in brake vans applied their handbrakes on hearing the special deep-toned whistle.) Speed was reduced, but the two engines collided causing two railwaymen and twelve passengers to be injured. Mr Wright, a commercial traveller 'opened his samples of wine and spirits and freely distributed them as restorates to the sufferers'. The injured were taken to the Bear Hotel, Chippenham. A guard died the following morning.

At the ensuing inquiry, the goods driver said that he had seen the distant signal against him, looked at the fire and then looked at the home signal and thought it showed clear. The Locomotive Superintendent at Swindon giving evidence said that if you looked at a bright fire for half a minute, you could not distinguish colours for two minutes. At the trial the driver was acquitted of manslaughter, but removed from the footplate.

On 16 January 1907 an almost exact re-enactment of this accident occurred. As the 5.05 p.m. goods from Swindon to Plymouth approached Thingley Junction, the driver, to his horror, saw the 6.30 p.m. passenger from Westbury to Chippenham crossing his path. In the smash the goods engine overturned and the wagons made two piles 50 ft high. The signalman at the adjacent box wired Chippenham to send a special with a doctor on board. The two injured locomen were laid on cushions in the brake van of this special train, taken to Chippenham and later carried on stretchers to the cottage hospital, the other injured walking. Both engines were so badly damaged that they were cut up on the spot. Fortunately the first two compartments of the first coach were locked – had they been occupied there would have been fatalities.

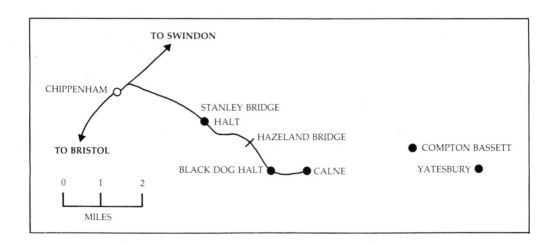

Auto train for Calne standing at platform 4, Chippenham. Headed by an 0–6–0PT, it consists of two trailer coaches. Left can be seen the stand on wheels used by the carriage cleaners.

M.E.J. Deane

The Family Train: driver Tom Smith, his son, fireman Kenneth Smith and daughter, guard Joan Smith, the youngest lady guard in Britain. The locomotive is 54xx class 0–6–0PT No. 5403 and is standing in the Calne bay platform. The photograph was specially posed, as, being an auto train, a bell, not flag, was used to signal departure.

Frank Cannon Collection

Two trains leaving Chippenham. On the left an unidentified 45xx class 2–6–2T leaves with the 10.23 a.m. to Calne, while No. 5077 *Eastnor Castle* is in charge of the 7.55 a.m. Taunton to Paddington. The SR cattle wagons are for beasts from Chippenham market.

1939   E.J.M. Hayward

An 0–6–0PT pushes the 5.35 p.m. Calne to Westbury auto by Chippenham East inner home. Behind the engine is a van of Harris & Co.'s products. Notice that trains from Calne have a fixed, not movable, distant signal. This is because some trains used the terminal bay. A check rail is on the tight curve. In the foreground, scrap rail has been cut ready for loading.

c. 1953   Roy Ball

Steam rail motor No. 19 arrives at Stanley Bridge with an 'Up' train. 'Halte' has the original spelling, soon modified by dropping the 'e'. Notice the cross slats on the platform ramp to avoid people slipping. The timber platform was later replaced by one of the solid variety.

c. 1905   Calne Town Council

45xx class 2–6–2T No. 5523 climbs the 1 in 80 gradient away from Stanley Bridge Halt with the 10.22 a.m. ex-Chippenham.

25.10.55   Author

The 12.54 p.m. from Chippenham to Calne hauled by 14xx class No. 1433, seen between Stanley Bridge and Black Dog Halts.

25.10.55   Author

14xx class 0–4–2T No. 1433 pushes the 1.12 p.m. from Calne – the return working of the 12.54 p.m. ex-Chippenham near Hazeland Bridge.

22.10.55   Author

Black Dog Halt in the 1930s as a private station, before receiving its nameboard. Notice the folded wagon sheet between the main line and siding.

P. Vines

A very crowded scene in Calne goods yard. The cattle vans had probably brought pigs for Messrs Harris. In 1906 the bank in the foreground was excavated to allow a further siding to be laid.

c. 1905   Author's Collection

Milk churns can be seen left, while the nearest part of Calne station building is the new parcels office extension, the platform canopy not yet having been extended in front of it. Advertisements on the walls publicize Newbury's furniture, carpets and curtains, also GWR sailings to Brest and Cork. Right is the GWR motor bus to Marlborough, a 20 hp Milnes Daimler No. 31, registration AX 120.

c. 1908   Author's Collection

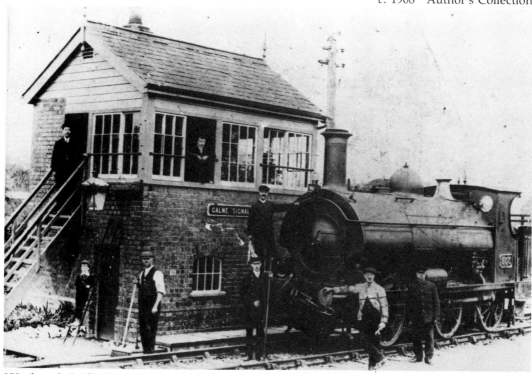

850 class 0–6–0ST No. 853 beside Calne signal-box. Signalman Arthur Gabb looks out of the window, his son stands on the window-cleaning ladder. George Jones in the permanent way packer and the fireman is Jim Fellander.

c. 1905   P. Vines Collection

70

A GWR boundary marker, dated 1889, near Stanley Bridge Halt. The cast-iron head, diameter 8 in and 3 in thick, was fixed when molten on a 4 ft length of rail weighing at least 60 lb/yd. A 12 in length of angle iron was riveted on its base to form an inverted 'T'. The rail and its base were then buried at least $2\frac{1}{2}$ ft into the ground. It proved an excellent and substantial design. The head is fixed too firmly to remove; the post too solid to break or bend; even if excavated the total of 100 lb is difficult to lift.

Author

Label from the Calne cash bag.

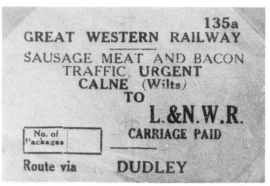

Sausage meat and bacon traffic label for use from Calne to the London & North Western Railway. Notice the rather unusual routing via Dudley.

Left: Selection of Calne branch tickets.
Ken Smith Collection

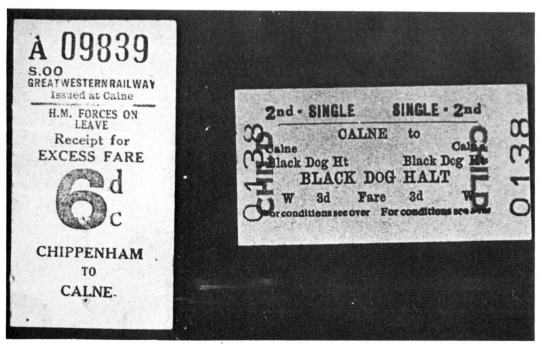

Selection of Calne branch tickets.

Michael Farr Collection

Loading branded vans at Calne under the station-master's supervision. The nearest boxes contain lard. Note the roof-board advertisement on each vehicle.

c. 1925   Edgar Gross

Inspecting the damage caused when a goods train smashed empty cattle vans against the blocks.

18.5.55   Mrs P. Gleed

Chippenham to Trowbridge

This length of track, originally the main line to Weymouth, became a branch in 1901 when Paddington to Weymouth trains were diverted to the new direct line built between Patney & Chirton and Westbury.

The story of the Chippenham to Trowbridge line, or more accurately Thingley Junction to Bradford Junction, began back in 1841 when the GWR was opened between London and Bristol. Three years later, the Wilts. & Somerset Railway was proposed to run from the main line at Corsham to Salisbury. Only a few months after this suggestion was made, the GWR felt that the line should be extended to Weymouth in order to cut off the advance of its rival, the London & South Western Railway, so 'Weymouth' was added to the title.

The Wilts., Somerset & Weymouth Railway received its Act in June 1845 but, unfortunately, in the slump which followed the Railway Mania, the WSWR found it difficult to raise the necessary finance. The directors believed that the wisest policy was to complete initially the Thingley to Westbury section as this was expected to be the most profitable length. To add to their difficulties, the contractor defaulted. Although the WSWR was floated as a nominally independent company, it was virtually a subsidiary of the GWR and was absorbed by the larger undertaking on 14 March 1850.

As was generally the custom, the directors made a trip on the line prior to the opening to the general public. The *Bath Chronicle* reported:

> On Saturday [2nd September 1848] the directors, accompanied by numerous friends, made an experimental trip on the line from Thingley to Westbury, preparatory to the opening for general traffic. At twelve o'clock a special left this city, drawn by the *Vulture* engine, which was driven by Mr Gooch, superintendent of the locomotive department of the GWR, assisted by Mr Brunel, engineer. At Melksham the train was received with loud cheering from the assembled populace, flags waving and bands of music playing. At Trowbridge also there was a great assemblage of people, and salutes of cannon were fired from the iron foundry. At Westbury, the Mayor presented the directors with a congratulatory address, to which a suitable reply was returned by the chairman of the board.

On 5 September 1848 the regular service of five trains each way and three on Sundays, began.

It is interesting to recall that Isambard Brunel, the line's engineer, had strong objections to facing points, especially away from stations where speed might be high, so at Thingley Junction trains had to stop and reverse into a siding before they could proceed to Melksham.

The line was built to the broad gauge and converted to standard gauge in June 1874. The operation was well planned. Platelayers had been drafted from other districts and conveyed in a special train. The men received 1s.3d. a day for rations and drank oatmeal and water sweetened with sugar. The GWR provided sheds for the men to sleep in, but little rest was taken, seventeen or eighteen hours being worked out of every twenty-four. The ballast had been cleared previously and the transoms partly sawn through so that when the engineers gained full possession of the line, the transoms could be completely sawn and the rail and baulk pushed to the narrower gauge and fastened. The 'Down' line from Thingley Junction to Westbury, and the 'Up' line from Bradford to Bradford Junction, were converted first on 16 June, a reduced service working on the other line. Early on Sunday 21 June, the last broad-gauge train left Frome and the 'Up' line to Thingley Junction was closed, all traffic using the newly-converted narrow-gauge line. The conversion was finished on 25 June.

The only original intermediate station was at Melksham. Holt was opened in 1861, but only as an exchange station, consisting of an island platform for passengers and parcels, to and from the Devizes branch until 1874 when it opened to the outside public. Lacock Halt opened on 16 October 1905, a fortnight after the introduction of the Trowbridge to Chippenham railmotor service. At first it had a low platform, the motors having retractable steps, but just before the First World War it was raised to standard height so that all trains could use it. It closed on 18 April 1966. Beanacre and Broughton Gifford Halts were both open from 29 October 1905 until 7 February 1955. Staverton Halt was in use for the same period as Lacock. The guard issued tickets at these four halts, and at Beanacre and Staverton he also had to lower steps due to the absence of standard height platforms. The retracting steps had to be unlocked with a carriage key and then a lever moved. It was essential that they were returned to their travelling position close to the coach side, or they fouled the next standard platform and were ripped off.

During the Second World War the War Department yard at Beanacre had exempted lighting. When a preliminary air-raid warning was received, normal lighting was switched off and blue lights turned on to assist shunting operations. During a raid, the engine spread out wagons loaded with TNT. Each wagon had to be separate from the next, because if one had been hit by the enemy, the rest would have exploded.

As the branch connected the Bristol to Reading and the Westbury to Reading lines, it proved useful as an alternative route in the event of one route being blocked during the Second World War. To increase its usefulness, an extra loop was laid at Thingley Junction to allow through running from Corsham to Lacock thus creating a triangular junction. Built at tax-payers' expense, it was Government, not GWR, property.

The local passenger service was withdrawn on 18 April 1966 and this marked the end of the Elizabethan-style stone station at Melksham designed by J. Geddes. The line was subsequently singled. Following Melksham's closure to passengers, normally there was only one passenger train in each direction, though on summer Saturdays the number increased as the line was used by through trains from the Midlands to Weymouth. After September 1971 the route was not used by trains on summer Saturdays until 1975 when the Weymouth to Manchester train worked over the branch. Then in 1981 the 09.45 Paddington to Penzance used a most curious route. After Thingley it passed through Melksham on its way to Salisbury where it reversed and travelled over the former Southern Railway line to Exeter where it regained the former GWR route. The summer of that same year saw the introduction of a Swindon, Westbury and Weymouth 'Sandhoppers' Train' on Mondays to Thursdays, this being the first local service over the Melksham line for fifteen years. Then on 13 May 1985 Melksham station re-opened to a limited Swindon to Westbury service.

Two accidents occurred to branch trains at Thingley Junction. The first was on to Calne or Stanley Bridge. Stanley Bridge halt was opened on 3 April 1905. Milk traffic here was so heavy that it took a quarter of an hour to load all the churns.

One of the mainstays of the branch was Harris's traffic from Calne. This was conveyed in vans with special enamel signs, which were cleaned daily by a carriage cleaner sent from Chippenham. These vans travelled to such places as London, Manchester, Newcastle upon Tyne, Portsmouth and Cardiff. Another big user of the line was the RAF, both equipment and personnel travelling by rail. The Air Ministry endeavoured to route personnel by rail as much as possible, but sometimes they overdid it. On one occasion a party from Compton Bassett to Lyneham travelled by coach from Compton Bassett to Calne, by rail from Calne to Dauntsey, and by coach from Dauntsey to Lyneham. This involved a rail journey of $11\frac{3}{4}$ miles plus 7 miles by road, against a direct road distance of 4 miles!

On Thursday evenings a member of the Calne station booking office staff travelled to Compton Bassett and another to the RAF station at Yatesbury on a railway lorry. To travel on this vehicle clerks had to hold a special pass. On arrival they sold tickets at the camps in order to avoid long queues forming at the station at weekends. This procedure allowed servicemen holding a pre-booked ticket to step straight on to a train. Each travelling booking clerk had a small case labelled 'Camp A' or 'Camp B' containing tickets for main destinations, blanks being made out for other places. The total collected from the two camps could sometimes amount to over £1,000 and it was said that on these occasions it was left overnight at Calne police station for safekeeping.

In both World Wars the branch carried heavy traffic and during the Second, the passenger platform at Calne was extended to accommodate an 8-coach train, essential as there were some 20,000 servicemen in the area.

Most of the steam locomotives on the line were replaced by diesels in 1958. Freight services were withdrawn in 1963, the year the Beeching Report recommended the branch's closure. A census taken during the week ending 10 October 1964 revealed that the average train carried only thirteen passengers and as the operation and maintenance of the branch was uneconomic, it closed, the last train running on 18 September 1965.

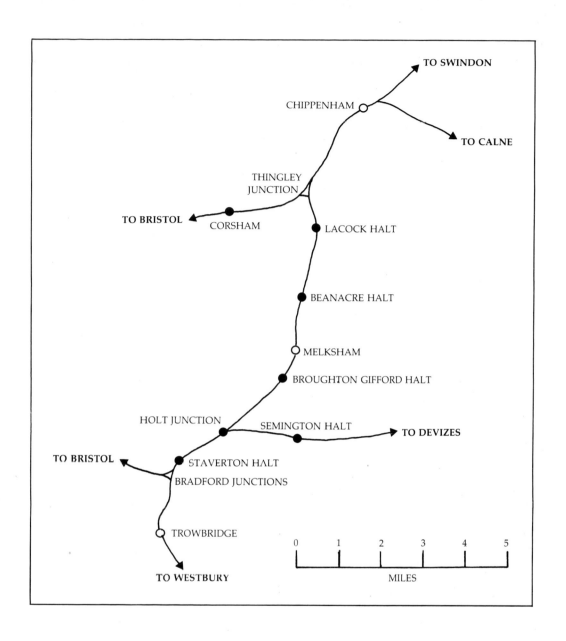

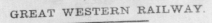

GREAT WESTERN RAILWAY.

NOTICE

OF

BALLASTING WITH AN ENGINE

BETWEEN

MELKSHAM AND YEOVIL

ON

MONDAYS, TUESDAYS, THURSDAYS & FRIDAYS,

UNTIL FURTHER NOTICE

To commence on TUESDAY, August 1st, 1865.

DOWN.			UP.		
Melksham ..	*dep.* 7	50 P.M.	Yeovil	*dep.* 12	0 A.M.
Holt Junction	" 8	0 "	Wells .. .. {pass about}		12 30 "
Trowbridge ..	" 8	10 "	Shepton Mallet	"	12 40 "
Westbury ..	" 8	25 "	Witham	"	12 55 "
Frome	*arr.* 8	45 "	Frome	*dep.* 1	10 "
"	*dep.* 8	50 "	Westbury ..	"	1 30 "
Witham.. ..	*arr.* 9	5 "	Trowbridge ..	"	1 45 "
Shepton Mallet	*dep.* 9	20 "	Holt Junction	"	1 55 "
Wells	*arr.* 9	45 "	Melksham ..	*arr.* 2	5 "

This Train must arrive punctually at Yeovil so as to be
clear of the Single Line before the arrival of the 9.0 p.m.
Up Goods, which leaves Yeovil at 11.20 p.m.

Frome must take care that the Ballast Train is clear of
the Line before the 1.30 a.m. Down Bristol Goods is permitted
to leave.

THOMAS GRAHAM,

Bristol, *July 29th,* 1865.   *Superintendent.*

ARROWSMITH, "Railway Guide Office," 11, Quay Street, Bristol.

Notice of ballasting between Melksham and Yeovil, 1 August 1865.

54xx class 0–6–0PT No. 5416 working a stopping train from Westbury, joins the Bristol to Swindon line at Thingley Junction. Notice the water tank with pump house below. This supplied water to engines using the Royal Naval and Air Ministry sidings at Thingley.

Trevor J. Saunders

A very rare photograph of a War Department 2–8–0, normally only used on goods trains, passing Thingley Junction with the 5.30 p.m. Westbury to Swindon parcels train. The marshalling sidings are beyond the bracket signal.

c. 1950   Trevor J. Saunders

The brand-new Railmotor No. 56 hauling a Siphon (milk van) at the opening of Lacock Halt. The presence of an 0–6–0ST at the rear is strange. It is quite possible that in view of the importance of the occasion and uncertainty of steaming with a new railmotor, a class not renowned for power or reliability, plus an added 'Siphon', additional steam power was provided as a safeguard. Notice that the platforms are low and only just above rail level. Some spectators watch the proceedings from an adjacent field.

16.10.05   Alan Newman Collection

An 'Up' train at Melksham.

c. 1909   Author's Collection

From the same viewpoint fifty years later. Spot the changes.

4.8.59   Author

Melksham station flooded.

June 1935   *Bath Evening Chronicle*

Avon India Rubber Co. Ltd's 10 ton coal wagon built by the Gloucester Railway Carriage & Wagon
Co. Ltd in April 1909. It was painted black, with white lettering.

Author's Collection

54xx class 0–6–0PT No. 5422 in GWR livery at Melksham, sandwiched between auto car W90 and an SR utility van. W90 was built in September 1912 at a cost of about £1,200. It was condemned in October 1956. A similar vehicle, No. 92, is preserved at Didcot by the Great Western Society.

c. 1950   Trevor J. Saunders

A picture from a similar viewpoint to that above showing the auto train's successor, a diesel multiple unit, the centre trailer buffet second-class coach of which is W59424. This 'Cross Country' unit was built by the Gloucester Railway Carriage & Wagon Co.

1965   D. Payne

Melksham, the view north, showing the substantial goods shed.

c. 1965   D. Payne

61xx class 2–6–2T No. 6169 in GWR livery with a ballast train at Melksham. It is on a 'running-in' turn ex-Swindon Works, as this class of engine was London Division allocated at this period.

Trevor J. Saunders

45xx class 2–6–2T No. 5523 in rather worn GWR livery at Melksham.

c. 1950   Trevor J. Saunders

28xx class 2–8–0 No. 3861 hauling empty stock at Melksham.

Trevor J. Saunders

Pressed Steel Co.'s three-car Suburban DMU B433 working the 7.32 a.m. Warminster to Gloucester. This was the first train to call at Melksham station when it was re-opened. A former station-master, Mr W. Clothier, performed the ceremony.

13.5.85   Author

2301 class 0–6–0 No. 2445 with mixed freight train near Melksham.

Trevor J. Saunders

43xx class 2–6–0 No. 5358 at Holt Junction with a 'Down' goods train from Thingley Junction.

Trevor J. Saunders

No. 4966 *Shakenhurst Hall* leaving Holt Junction with an 'Up' stopping passenger train to the Devizes line. Shadows indicate that it is probably the 1.45 p.m. Weston-super-Mare to Reading.

Trevor J. Saunders

BR Standard class 4 MT 4–6–0 No. 75007 passing Holt Junction with a 'Down' express. The coach roof boards and 'A' class express headlamps suggest the 11.15 a.m. Wolverhampton to Weymouth.

Trevor J. Saunders

Derby Works Suburban DMU consisting of Motor Brake Second W51136 and Motor Second W51149 and intermediate trailer, working the 4.15 p.m. Chippenham to Westbury away from Staverton Halt, just visible behind the overbridge.

4.8.59   Author

A 'Down' two-coach auto train being propelled near Bradford Junctions. Notice the warning bell outside the driver's vestibule. The other line has a trap point to derail a runaway in the wrong direction.

Trevor J. Saunders

An 0–4–2T pushing two auto trailers near Bradford Junctions: an original GWR vehicle and its BR development.

Trevor J. Saunders

A 14xx class 0–4–2T hauling a BR auto trailer near Bradford Junctions.

Trevor J. Saunders

A War Department 2–8–0 hauling a mixed freight near Bradford Junctions.

Trevor J. Saunders

Because of the ever present risk of accident, many railwaymen were fully qualified amublance-men. Here the Melksham GWR ambulance corps has a decorated float complete with patient on a stretcher, outside the goods shed. The team is, by the horse: J. Missen, D. Taylor, O. Drew. At the back: F. King, B. Moore, C. Gillette, J. Scally, B. Vincent, R. Hunt. On the stretcher is D. Fletcher and F. Toop stands. Mr Drew was later station-master at Trowbridge. The left-hand poster reads 'Safety First. Don't argue. Under slung timber on you might get a little +'. The other says 'A friend in need'.

1926   Author's Collection

Holt to Patney & Chirton

The line from Holt to Patney was built in two sections: Devizes being approached first from the west and then from the east.

The story started back in June 1845 when the Wilts., Somerset & Weymouth Railway received an Act to build a line from Chippenham to Weymouth, with several branches, one of which was from Melksham to Devizes. An Act the following year altered the junction to Holt. The company ran into financial difficulties and was taken over by the GWR. At last on 1 July 1857, more than twelve years after the Act had been passed, the line between Holt and Devizes was opened. There were no intermediate stations. The press announced that the opening was 'a full week earlier than expected so that there was no time to organize the customary celebrations'. At Holt an island platform had been constructed between the 'Up' and 'Down' lines and the *Devizes Gazette* reported that '. . . hundreds flocked to the station to see the first train leave at 7.45 a.m. and many spent the entire day travelling backwards and forwards between Devizes and Holt for the sheer joy of it'. Seend station opened in September 1858. A year before the branch opened, the Great Western Iron Ore Smelting Company had acquired 15 acres of land about a quarter of a mile west of the village. Unfortunately for the railway's economy, this iron ore company went bankrupt in 1859. The workings were sold several times, but were hardly a success. During the First World War production increased and an overhead cable conveyed ore to the station in large steel buckets.

On 11 November 1862 the Berks. & Hants. Extension Railway was opened from Hungerford to Devizes giving direct access from Devizes to Reading. This meant that the Devizes line could be used as an alternative route from Bath to London and this proved useful on several occasions, especially when there were occasional falls of rock in Box Tunnel.

In addition to semi-fast services between Reading, Newbury, Bristol and Weston-super-Mare, for a considerable period a regular express ran in each direction from Bristol to London via Devizes, hauled by a 'Castle' or 'Hall' class locomotive. The Devizes branch experienced busy traffic during the Tidworth Tattoo, heavy excursion trains being worked through from South Wales and Bristol. To encourage traffic over the Devizes line, unstaffed halts were opened at Semington on 3 August 1907 and at Bromham & Rowde on 22 February 1909.

The branch crossed the Melksham to Devizes road by the 'fish bridge', so called because the first bridge of 110 ft span consisted of wrought iron flange-type girders very much like the skeleton of a fish. In 1901 this original bridge was replaced by a steel braced-girder type. Devizes station was quite impressive with three platforms, and, until rebuilt around the turn of the century, covered by an overall train shed. Beyond was the 190 yd long tunnel. Pans Lane Halt, originally Pans Lane Bridge Halt, opened on 4 March 1929 to serve the hospital. As the platform was only 208 ft in length, passengers wishing to get out were required to travel in the rear coaches of the train. It closed on 6 October 1941, though trains still continued to call when required.

91

With the development of road transport, traffic on the Devizes line declined to such an extent that it was no longer economic so services were withdrawn on 18 April 1966, track being lifted the following year.

Just over a century ago, the Devizes branch was the scene of an attempted murder. Shortly after 1.30 p.m. platelayer Burgess was working on the line just below the Fish Bridge. The 11.10 a.m. stopping train from Reading to Trowbridge approached and, looking into a third class compartment as it went by, Burgess was horrified to see a woman stand and suddenly throw up both arms. A man in the compartment with her fired two shots from a revolver and pushed her out of the carriage window. George Williams, a plasterer working on a cottage near the bridge, heard a shout as the train passed and, looking round, saw a woman hanging out of the window and then falling on to the embankment. Both he and Burgess ran to her. They found a well-dressed woman lying fully conscious, but bleeding profusely. They carried her to Devizes Cottage Hospital.

She was not the only casualty that afternoon. Shortly after, a man's mangled corpse was discovered on the embankment a quarter of a mile west of the scene of the first incident. This body was conveyed to Devizes Workhouse.

It transpired that the woman was Miss Emily Lister, headmistress of Devizes British School who had taken up her new post only a month previously. Aged about twenty-nine, she was the daughter of W. Lister, a Birmingham oil merchant. Her mother, until 1880, had kept a private school in King Edward's Road, Birmingham. Emily had previously taught at Connaught Road Board School, Brighton. The deceased man was Augustus George Keeling. Aged about twenty-seven, he had been a pupil teacher at the South Metropolitan District Schools, Sutton, Surrey. A brilliant musician and athelete, his conduct had been erratic at the Teachers' Training College at Exeter. On one occasion during a service in the cathedral, he mounted the steps into the pulpit and it was only with great difficulty that he was persuaded to leave. He was sent to a private asylum, but left after a brief stay because his conduct had improved.

Augustus, head over heels in love with Emily, had followed her from Brighton and applied for a post of assistant master at her school. He had been staying at Devizes for a week trying to win her affections and on the morning of the tragedy, had tried to induce her to walk down a lonely lane near the town, but she refused. Embarrassed by the situation, she tried to get away from Devizes. Taking advantage of the Whitsun half term holiday, she decided to return to her parents at Birmingham.

Reaching the station, she did not expect him to board the train. Then, as it left, having bought a ticket to Seend, he jumped in at the last moment and asked her to give him money. When she refused, he leapt up, caught her by the hair and, as the train rumbled over the Fish Bridge, fired two shots with a revolver. When she put her head out of the window to shout for assistance, he took her by the feet and pushed her out of the window. Fortunately for Emily, the shots had struck the only parts of the skull that were difficult to penetrate, both bullets flattening against the bone.

A Mr Brice travelling in an adjoining compartment, saw Keeling aiming a revolver at Emily and as the train was not equipped with a communication cord, daringly opened the compartment door and stepped out on to the carriage footboard in order to reach the guard. Inspector Upchurch of Reading, seeing him outside the coach, stopped the train near the gate to Seend brickyard.

One of Emily's eyeballs was crushed when she fell from the train and had to be removed by surgery. Three days after her terrifying experience on the train she was able to talk. Unaware of the death of Augustus, she expressed a hope that he would be dealt with leniently.

Four days after the incident, Augustus Keeling was buried at the expense of the parish. He was certainly something of a mystery man. None of his relatives came forward. His hat had been bought in New York and his revolver in Paris. As two pawn tickets were found in his pockets in different names, it was suspected that he could have been using an assumed designation. The coroner returned an open verdict to the cause of his death, but it was believed that he fell under the train when jumping off to escape capture.

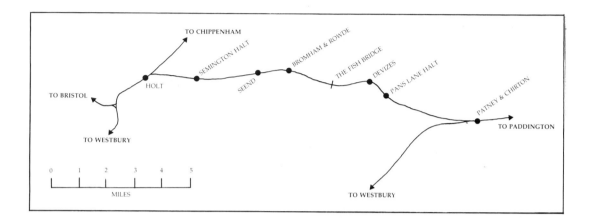

Holt Junction, view north. A 4-4-0 hauls a train of three or four coaches. The single island platform is unusual for the GWR, access being across the footbridge. The card is postmarked 23 December 1905.

Paul Strong Collection

The fireman of a train to the Devizes line seizes the single line tablet as his train curves away from Holt Junction. The horn of the setting-down post for receiving the tablet from trains on the other direction can be seen just beyond the netting.

Trevor J. Saunders

No. 6968 *Woodcock Hall* approaches Holt Junction with a stopping train from the Berks. and Hants. via Devizes. Notice the spare headlamp in front of the first splasher and 'B' set next to the tender.

Trevor J. Saunders

The fireman of an 'Up' train collecting the staff at Seend for the single line ahead to Devizes. The signal-post is made of concrete and manufactured at the company's concrete works, Taunton. The holes were to make the post lighter.

Trevor J. Saunders

A 'Hall' class 4–6–0 heading a 'Down' train crosses the Kennet & Avon Canal east of Bromham & Rowde Halt.

Trevor J. Saunders

No. 4085 *Berkeley Castle* stands at Seend with a 'Down' stopping train, while an 'Up' train departs. The station is signalled for two-way working so that a single line can be used when the signal-box is switched out.

Trevor J. Saunders

View of Seend station through the cab window of a DMU following the lifting of the 'Down' track.
D. Payne

No. 4959 *Purley Hall* coupled to a Hawksworth tender, leaving Seend with an 'Up' train. Levers of the ground frame can be seen on the right.

Trevor J. Saunders

Bromham & Rowde Halt shortly after it was opened on 22 February 1909. Notice the looped siding beyond. This was an unusual feature at the halt, but it is evident that it saw considerable traffic.

Paul Strong Collection

Traffic at Bromham & Rowde Halt grew to such an extent that additional shelter was required and a porter kept in attendance in the wooden hut, left, but he was withdrawn from 5 November 1951.

29.9.62   Author

The 3.35 p.m. Westbury to Newbury crosses the Kennet & Avon Canal east of Bromham & Rowde Halt and climbs the 1 in 93 gradient towards Devizes. The locomotive is probably No. 6982 *Melmerby Hall*.

c. 1964   Paul Strong

A 'Pannier' tank engine, probably No. 7764, hauls an 'Up' freight at the same location.

Trevor J. Saunders

The replacement 'Fish Bridge' looking up Caen Hill towards Devizes. This card is postmarked 9 September 1908.

Paul Strong Collection

Devizes station before the removal of the overall roof. A railmotor, or auto trailer, stands on the left.

c. 1905   Author's Collection

An 0–6–0ST in charge of an 'Up' goods. Notice the track on longitudinal sleepers.

c. 1905   Paul Strong Collection

A train carrying Second World War Army ambulances and lorries at Devizes.

Author's Collection

No. 7914 *Lleweni Hall* with a 'Down' stopping passenger to Trowbridge, leaving the castellated mouth of Devizes tunnel and about to enter Devizes station.

Trevor J. Saunders

Modified 'Hall' No. 6959 *Peatling Hall* leaving Devizes with the 3.15 p.m. Westbury to Reading train.

21.3.64   Hugh Ballantyne

Two DMUs cross at Devizes. On the left, the 8.00 a.m. Devizes to Warminster, on the right, the 6.58 a.m. Trowbridge to Reading, the destination line of which reads 'Paddington'

June 1965   Paul Strong

A 57xx class 0–6–0PT leaving Devizes tunnel with a 'Down' goods train and entering the station.
Trevor J. Saunders

Devizes station from the cab of a 'Down' DMU about to emerge from the tunnel. This view was taken after closure of the signal-box on 4 July 1965 which explains the de-armed signal and shortened goods lines, left.
Trevor J. Saunders

An 0–6–0PT leaving the castellated east mouth of Devizes tunnel with an 'Up' stopping train comprising a 'B' set. Notice the railwaymen's allotments on both sides of the line. These were very popular as they provided fresh vegetables for the family at minimal cost.

Trevor J. Saunders

28xx class 2–8–0 No. 2811 leaving Devizes tunnel with the 10.40 a.m. Saturdays-only Bristol to Reading. It was unusual to roster this class of engine on a passenger train, but it was done occasionally at weekends when they were surplus to freight demand and there was a shortage of power for passenger traffic.

17.8.57   Trevor J. Saunders

No. 5973 *Rolleston Hall* heads a 'Down' express into Devizes tunnel.

Trevor J. Saunders

A 'Down' train passing what was later to become the site of Pans Lane Halt. The large building on the skyline is the Wilts. United Dairies. The track is the old baulk road. The distant signal for Devizes can be seen just beyond the hut.

c. 1905   Author's Collection

The neatly kept Pans Lane Halt, view towards Patney & Chirton. The platform is of earth held in place by a wall of sleepers. Notice the allotments on the right.

Trevor J. Saunders

A DMU drawing into Devizes with a 'Down' train.

1965   D. Payne

An 'Up' DMU W51383 leaving Devizes and about to enter the tunnel. This Motor second-class car, built by the Pressed Steel Company, is of the Suburban type. Side doors are fitted at each seating bay in order to keep platform time to a minimum.

1965   P. Strong

A train from Newbury to Westbury via Devizes climbing away from the West of England main line west of Patney.

Trevor J. Saunders

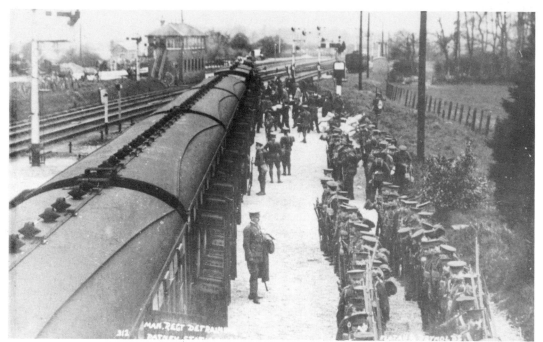

The 6th Manchester Regiment detraining at Patney & Chirton for West Down, South Camp, Salisbury Plain.

1910   Paul Strong Collection

Patney & Chirton looking west. An 'Up' DMU is on the main line on the left; a Devizes branch DMU on the right.

c. 1965   D. Payne

A view west from Patney & Chirton showing the Devizes branch running parallel with the main line.

c. 1965   D. Payne

Alf Harris, a DMU driver, receiving the single-line staff from the signalman at Patney & Chirton signal-box. Beyond the box the DMU will cross the 'Up' main line to the Devizes branch.
A. Harris Collection

The glistening interior of Patney & Chirton signal-box on the last day of working over the Devizes branch. The signal-box itself closed less than three months later on 6 July 1966.

16.4.66   Paul Strong

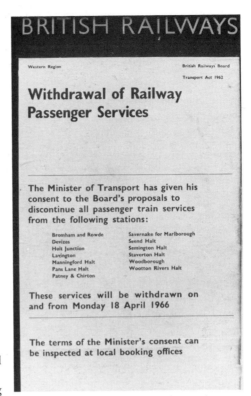

The writing on the wall for the Devizes branch and other small stations in the area.

Paul Strong

The very last train on the Devizes branch, the 7.36 p.m. Newbury to Westbury, arriving at Holt junction. The signalman has been handed the tablet.

16.4.66   Paul Strong

Corsham to Quarry Tunnel

The construction of Box tunnel revealed the extent of the beds of building stone and led to its exploitation by mining. It was a great advantage that the natural dip of the stone beds reached the level of the main GWR line near the eastern portal of Box tunnel. When Tunnel Quarry opened in 1844, immediately adjacent to the eastern entrance of the GWR's tunnel, a broad-gauge siding actually went into the hillside to ease the removal of the stone. Within the quarry tunnel, loaded narrow-gauge wagons descended by gravity to the broad-gauge exchange sidings, horses hauling wagons uphill and on the flat.

By 1862 no less than five miles of tunnels, equipped with tramways, fanned out from this main tunnel. In 1864 100,000 tons of stone left Corsham station. Locally the stone cost 6d. per cubic foot, transportation only raising it to 1s. 4d. at Plymouth, 1s. 5d. at Birmingham and 1s. 7d. at Newcastle upon Tyne. Around 1900, two trains of block stone left Corsham daily.

When the broad gauge was converted to standard gauge in 1875, this allowed room for a $\frac{3}{4}$ mile long siding to be laid parallel with the main line from Corsham station into Tunnel Quarry. Then, following the closure of Box Tunnel East signal-box on 24 June 1910, access was solely from Corsham, whereas until that date, there had been direct access to the 'Up' main line near the mouth of Box tunnel.

In 1936 the War Department took over Tunnel Quarry for ammunition storage and aircraft production, a private siding agreement dated 16 March 1938 being made with the GWR. The tons of soil, debris and in-fill cleared from the underground workings were used to form the foundation of sidings at Thingley Junction. The WD introduced standard gauge underground diesel locomotives built to a restricted loading gauge. The first was 0–6–0 Hunslet, works No. 1846, with an eight-cylinder Gardner engine giving 204 b.h.p. at 1200 r.p.m. which at the time was the largest locomotive ever made for underground work. The exhaust was conditioned by passing it through water in order to prevent the aldehydes causing acute irritation of eyes and nose. In 1939 two John Fowler & Co. diesel-mechanical 0–4–0s joined No. 1, followed by two more Hunslets in 1940. These latter two remained to work the system until its closure about 1963, when the locomotives were taken to the Bicester workshops where they were rebuilt to normal loading gauge. The private siding agreement was officially terminated on 24 November 1967 and the line to Tunnel Quarry lifted in March 1973.

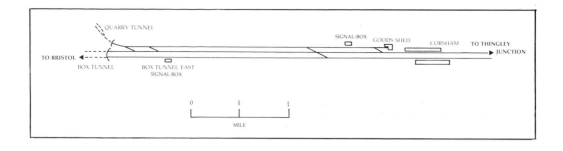

An 'Up' express hauled by a 4–2–2 locomotive, leaves the east end of Box tunnel. Right is the smaller, lower tunnel leading to the stone quarries. The quarry line is laid on longitudinal baulks, unlike the more modern main line track which has cross sleepers. The card was postmarked 9 August 1904.

Author's Collection

Entrance to the Box tunnels. On the left is the main line, the quarry tunnel on the right, with wagons of stone blocks awaiting collection. Since the previous photograph, a fence and gate separate the quarry company's land from that of the railway. The card is postmarked 26 June 1915.

Author's Collection

A further view of the two tunnels. A stone wagon awaits collection, right, while 'Saint' class 4–4–2 No. 182 *Lalla Rookh* emerges with an 'Up' express. Built in June 1905, it was re-numbered No. 2982 in 1906 and converted to a 4–6–0 wheel arrangement in November 1912. It was withdrawn from service in June 1934. The route of the lower section of the flight of steps has been modified.

c. 1910   Author's Collection

The line in front of the signal-box at Corsham station led to quarry tunnel.

c. 1910   Author's Collection

Stone wagons at Corsham. The line in the foreground led to Tunnel Quarry.

c. 1910   Author's Collection

Grateley to Bulford and Associated Military Lines

When the War Office decided to establish a permanent military site on Salisbury Plain, the London & South Western Railway applied for a Light Railway Order to build the Amesbury & Military Camp Light Railway. Powers were granted on 28 September 1898, land subsequently purchased and the contract for construction let to Messrs J.T. Firbank. Although authorized as a 'light railway', unlike most other light railways it had heavy engineering works, rather than following the lie of the land. Track was laid with 87 1b/yd bull-head rail rather than flat-bottom rail spiked directly to the sleepers and sufficient land had been purchased to lay double track. Embankments varied from about 10 to 35 ft in height and the cuttings from 8 to 38 ft in depth. The layout at Grateley station on the main line was remodelled, the principal alteration being that the existing 'Up' platform was made into an island, Amesbury branch trains using its outer face.

The branch to Amesbury was opened to military traffic on 1 October 1901, to goods traffic on 26 April, and public passengers on 2 June – the first train of the day bringing the morning papers with the joyful news that the South African War was over.

A Light Railway Order of 10 January 1903 authorized an extension from Amesbury to the recently-built camps at Bulford and Sling. This section was constructed, rather unusually, by the LSWR's own staff instead of employing an outside contractor. This extension was opened for public passenger services to Bulford on 1 June 1906.

In the meantime, the LSWR applied for a Light Railway Order to make a junction near Newton Tony to give a direct run to Salisbury, the existing junction only giving a through run to the east. In order to avoid a train from Amesbury to Salisbury fouling an 'Up' main-line train, the 'Down' branch line burrowed under the main tracks. At the same time as this junction was made, the branch was doubled as far as Newton Tony station. These works were opened to passengers on 8 August 1904. To facilitate the heavy traffic caused by army manoeuvres, the double line was extended to Bulford on 23 May 1909. Amesbury in its heyday was quite an impressive station with three spacious platforms allowing plenty of room for loading and unloading troops, while in addition were three lengthy loading docks. To enable tender engines to be used on the branch, the goods yard had a turntable. Bulford was a much simpler layout with only one platform and a passing loop.

With the outbreak of the First World War further camps sprang up, these being served by the Larkhill Military Railway which curved away westwards from the Bulford line midway between Amesbury and Bulford. It ran to Larkhill and Rollestone, with branches to Flying Shed sidings and Fargo Hospital, the latter line finally terminating at Lake Down Airfield, Druid's Lodge. The Larkhill Military Railway was not worked by the LSWR but by the Southern Command of the Military Camp Railways. It opened in 1914 and closed in October 1929. The locomotive shed was between the junction with the Amesbury & Bulford line at Ratfyn and the viaduct over the Avon. A reversing triangle midway between the level crossing at Countess and Larkhill Camp enabled an engine to be turned without the use of a turntable. West of Larkhill Camp was a junction where a branch continued on to Rollestone Camp, where a balloon school was situated, the main line turning south to Fargo Hospital. Two branches off this line served the Handley Page aircraft hangars and Stonehenge Airfield, the main line terminating at Lake Down Airfield. The section from Lake Down, Stonehenge Airfield and Fargo Hospital closed in 1923. Midway between Newton Tony and Amesbury a short branch led to Boscombe Down Camp and was used 1917–18 for carrying materials for constructing an airfield.

During the Second World War the Amesbury & Bulford line became very busy, but no extensive branches were added as during the First World War.

In the late 1940s seven passenger trains ran in each direction daily between Salisbury and Bulford, while on Sunday evenings a through train from Waterloo was provided for soldiers returning from weekend leave. However, 1951 saw this cut back to one solitary train from Bulford to Salisbury and back. Even this sparse passenger service was withdrawn on 30 June 1952, goods traffic ceasing on 4 March 1963. The double track portions of the branch were singled in 1953/4.

In the early days branch passenger trains were worked by 0–4–4Ts and 0–4–2 tender engines, 0–6–0s handling freight traffic. In later years larger engines appeared, only 4–6–0s and 'Merchant Navy' class Pacifics being banned.

Not linked with the Bulford branch, but less than a couple of miles away at its nearest point, was another military line. This ran from transfer sidings in the goods yard of Porton station on the LSWR's Andover to Salisbury line, to Porton Camp 1½ miles north east of the station.

This 600 mm gauge line was laid in 1916 to Porton Camp, and opened as a trench warfare experimental station of the Royal Engineers. About half a mile from Porton station an extremely sinuous branch ran to Winterbourne Gunner Camp. This line was lifted by 1925, but the Porton Camp line continued in use until about 1950.

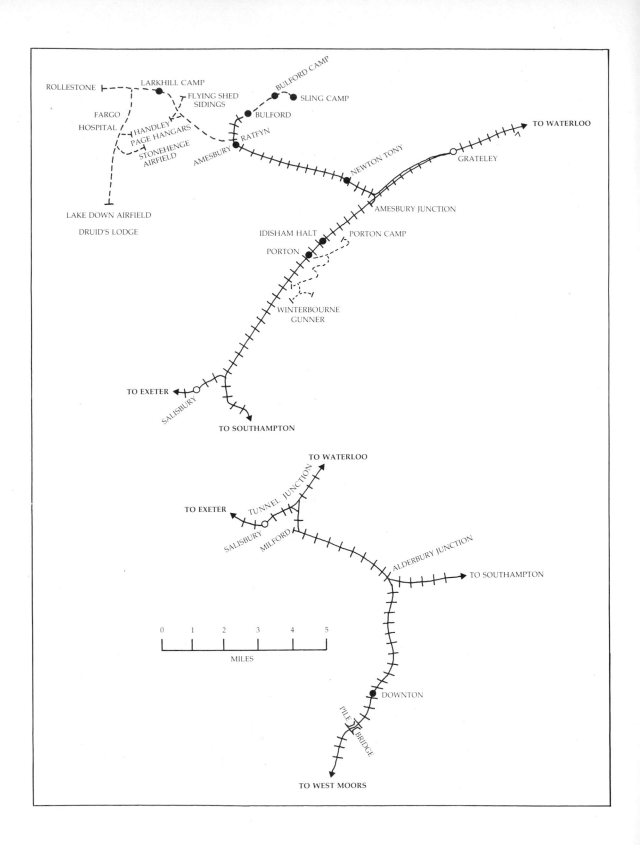

ROLLESTONE

LARKHILL CAMP

BULFORD CAMP

FLYING SHED
SIDINGS

SLING CAMP

FARGO
HOSPITAL

BULFORD

HANDLEY
PAGE HANGARS

RATFYN

STONEHENGE
AIRFIELD

AMESBURY

TO WATERLOO

NEWTON TONY

GRATELEY

LAKE DOWN AIRFIELD

AMESBURY JUNCTION

DRUID'S LODGE

IDISHAM HALT

PORTON CAMP

PORTON

WINTERBOURNE
GUNNER

TO EXETER

SALISBURY

TO SOUTHAMPTON

TO WATERLOO

TUNNEL JUNCTION

TO EXETER

SALISBURY

MILFORD

ALDERBURY JUNCTION

TO SOUTHAMPTON

0 1 2 3 4 5

MILES

DOWNTON

PILE BRIDGE

TO WEST MOORS

The former Amesbury Junction, and the view 'Up' showing the main line and the formation of the former Bulford branch which curved left beyond the overbridge and tunnelled below the main line. Following the closure of this spur, the signal-box was renamed 'Allington' until its closure on 20 January 1964.

c. 1964   Lens of Sutton

Newton Tony, with the view 'Up' showing the sleeper-faced gravel platforms. Left is the corrugated-iron goods shed, with corrugated-iron office building beyond and its adjacent signal-box.

Author's Collection

In this view looking towards Bulford, the former corrugated-iron administrative block has been rebuilt and its walls rendered. Notice the step midway along the platform making it easier for station staff to cross from one platform to the other. The signal-box has been replaced.

Author's Collection

Disused station and signal-box at Newton Tony following the withdrawal of the passenger service and the singling and slewing of track. Notice that the platform edging has been replaced by concrete slabs manufactured at the SR's concrete works at Exmouth Junction.

c. 1964   Lens of Sutton

A busy scene at Amesbury. A troop train has arrived drawn by two locomotives, the pilot running tender-first. Over on the right stand horse boxes, while this side of them are several carriage trucks. Notice the tops of the oil lamps set between the coach roof ventilators.

c. 1914   Lens of Sutton

A quieter scene at Amesbury, view towards Newton Tony. Taken after the withdrawal of the passenger service, the platforms are grass covered. A BR Bedford delivery lorry stands on the right. The 'Up' platform canopy has been removed, but the one on the 'Down' built from scaffolding poles in 1943, is retained.

Lens of Sutton

The single platform at Bulford, looking towards the Camp. The signal-box on the platform was reduced to a ground frame on 9 April 1935.

Author's Collection

The spacious platform at Bulford Camp, with an enthusiasts' train at the platform headed by 0298 class 2–4–0WT No. 30587.

14.5.55   Lens of Sutton

King George V and Queen Mary accompanied by Lord Kitchener leave Larkhill after inspecting Canadian troops. The soldiers are waving their caps.

1915   Paul Strong Collection

Salisbury, Alderbury Junction to Downton, the Milford Goods Branch, and Salisbury Market House Railway

The first line to reach Salisbury was that from Eastleigh, then called Bishopstoke, and was the remains of an abortive attempt by the LSWR to reach Bristol. On 27 January 1847 'Bison' class 0–6–0 No. 52 *Rhinoceros* under the charge of the driver of the Royal train, ran into the Milford terminus, Salisbury, with twenty-three wagons. The ensuing opening ceremony was unusual. Performed by W.J. Chaplin, chairman of the LSWR and elected MP for the city only two days before, he distributed 50 tons of coal among the poor, which arrived by this first train, another 50 tons arriving the following day. The line opened to passengers on 1 March the same year.

When the line from Andover to Salisbury opened on 1 May 1857, considerably shortening the distance to London, it too used Milford, but when the Salisbury & Yeovil Railway opened from Gillingham on 2 May 1859 a new spur connected Milford Junction and Tunnel Junction, all passenger trains from then on using a new station built on the new line which became a through route to the West. On the same date that this station opened, Milford closed to passenger traffic, but remained opened for freight. A busy yard, an engine was kept shunting continuously throughout twenty-four hours. The depot closed and all sidings were taken out of use at Milford on 21 August 1967.

From Alderbury Junction, 4 miles south of Salisbury on the Eastleigh line, a branch ran to West Moors, east of Wimborne, only the first section from Alderbury to Downton being in Wiltshire. This railway came about as a result of a meeting held at Salisbury on 20 October 1860 when support was given to build the Salisbury & Dorset Joint Railway to link with the Southampton & Dorchester Railway at Wimborne. It received its Act in 1861, and 3 February 1864 saw a cheerful crowd watch Countess Nelson ceremonially cut the first sod at Downton. The contractors, Garrett & Co., were replaced in September 1864 by Henry Jackson. Financial difficulties, coupled with the unusually wet winter of 1865–6 delayed the line's completion. When Captain Tyler made his inspection he found that works were below the recently-raised standard required for railways, but fortunately for the company, Jackson generously made these improvements at cost price. Eventually Tyler passed the line.

The opening day was 20 December 1866. Bells pealed at Salisbury, costing the directors four guineas. The new line hardly proved to be a roaring success. The LSWR, which worked the line, was only able to hand over £14 to the Salisbury company in the first six months as its share of the income. However, receipts rose from £4,981 in 1868 to

£8,893 in 1875. Unfortunately the LSWR proved most obstructive and did its best to dissuade passengers from travelling over the Salisbury & Dorset. It was certainly in its interest to do so as it received more income if passengers travelled further via the LSWR's own metals. One ploy was to use uncomfortable 'very old and very small carriages', while another was Waterloo booking clerks refusing to issue tickets via that line. As the Salisbury & Dorset failed to show the handsome returns its shareholders were anticipating, they sold it to the LSWR in January 1883.

The single-track branch was worked on the train tablet system and enginemen were specifically warned to reduce speed when giving up the tablet at Alderbury Junction, the signalman there having been injured as a result of exchange at high speed. As there was no scheduled stop at Alderbury and the distance from Downton to Salisbury was $8\frac{3}{4}$ miles there was a great temptation for drivers to run fast.

In 1922 economies were made at Downton, when on 1 December the 'Down' loop was converted into a siding and the signal-box closed and made into a ground frame. In November 1936 in connection with a pig marketing scheme, a new dock and pens were provided in the goods yard, an existing siding being slewed to serve it.

Some trains on the branch were push-and-pull operated. In addition to the normal traffic, the line was used on summer Saturdays in the 1950s by through Bournemouth to Cardiff trains and vice-versa.

Alderbury Junction was simply a junction and had no public platforms, passengers having to change at Salisbury, but at the junction staff platforms, not available for public use, were served by trains until the branch closed on 4 May 1964.

In due course the track was lifted. This was thirsty work and at the end of a hard day it was not unknown for men to ride on the contractor's locomotive from Fordingbridge along the line towards Alderbury Junction, there to catch a bus into Salisbury for a drink.

Over a century ago a railway disaster took place near Downton. On 3 June 1884 the 4.33 p.m. passenger train from Salisbury to Wimborne was well filled with folk returning from Salisbury market. It consisted of four-wheeled vehicles: guard's vans being at the front and rear with two first-class and four third-class coaches between. At its head were two locomotives – No. 294 a 2–4–0 of the 'Vesuvius' class, with 'Lion' class 0–6–0 No. 113 *Stour* coupled in front because No. 294 had steamed so poorly earlier that day.

The train left Salisbury station promptly. After a brief stop at Downton it proceeded on its way, a slight down gradient aiding acceleration, the fall increasing half a mile beyond the platforms to 1 in 78 for a quarter of a mile. Then followed a level stretch of line and an S-bend, with Pile Bridge over the Avon in the centre. Two hundred yards beyond the bridge, disaster struck – the train was derailed before taking the second curve. The two engines kept to the rails, except for the tender of No. 294, but the couplings parted behind the leading brake van and the train bumped along the permanent way for 100 yd before plunging over the embankment down 12 ft to a muddy ditch filled with 4 ft of water.

The coaches struck a willow tree, knocking it over, but it absorbed some of the shock. The two first-class coaches were completely smashed. The rear brake van lay on its side above a third-class coach which has both ends stove in, though the centre remained intact. Three females were killed: one was the fourteen-year-old daughter of the Fordingbridge station-master. Two of the three met their death by drowning. Two men were also killed, one dying next day in Salisbury Infirmary.

Professor Wright, his son and the forty students at the Downton College of Agriculture, opposite the scene of the accident, aided the rescue attempts. Twenty of the injured were conveyed to the college and six more sent to Salisbury Infirmary. The cries and shrieks of the wounded were said to be 'heart rending'. A total of forty-one passengers were injured. The rails of the permanent way were 'twisted about like pieces of wire'.

The LSWR directors sent a message to Salisbury: 'Mr Wyndham Portal and Colonel Campbell desire those in the Infirmary should be informed that the Queen has telegraphed from Balmoral expressing anxiety to know how the poor sufferers from the accident are progressing.'

William Witt, gatekeeper at Charford crossing beyond Downton, said that the coaches were oscillating as they passed him and appeared to be running into one another prior to the accident. He did not consider that the speed of the train was greater than usual, whereas James Porton, a shepherd, said that the train appeared to be moving faster than he had ever seen it before. John Hobbs, a well sinker of Wood Green, who actually witnessed the accident, said that the train was not going fast. Henry Colson, Permanent Way Inspector, reported that he had examined the line four days before the accident and found it in perfect order. This evidence conflicted with that given by Constance Hill, daughter of the Rector of Downton, who found that many keys had fallen out of the chairs holding the rails in place, and this would have been liable to render the gauge incorrect. Colonel Rich, the Board of Trade inspecting officer, said that the train had averaged 44 m.p.h. instead of 35 m.p.h. and locomotive No. 294 was dangerously unsteady and such a poor steamer that it could not exceed 28–30 m.p.h. on level track. Time could only be kept by speeding dangerously down inclines at 65–70 m.p.h. and this on track consisting of 70 lb/yd rails held in 22½ lb cast-iron chairs, which Colonel Rich said were too weak for such speeds. Rich censured the LSWR in his accident report:

> . . . the numerous complaints which have been made, and the violent shaking which passengers experienced when travelling on parts of the London & South Western Railway, leave no room to doubt that a great deal of reform in the management, and improvement in the working of this railway is required. I believe the complaints are caused in a great measure by bad driving, using inferior stock, and by the coaches in the trains not being properly coupled up. I would strongly urge the company to make a thorough examination of their system and stock, to classify their drivers, to classify their stock, to classify their several lines and parts of their system, and to classify their trains. It cannot be expected that the whole of a company's stock and railway shall be of the best description; but the public has a right to expect, that old and inferior stock shall not be run over old, weak, and inferior parts of the railway, at such speed as to make it unpleasant and dangerous to all that use it.

To prevent a repetition of the accident, on 20 August management sent out instructions severely restricting speeds on twenty lines and accordingly adjusting timetables, until track strengthening work, at once begun, was completed.

Twenty years later, Downton was again the scene of an accident. On 2 November 1904 the 4.50 p.m. goods from Wimborne arrived at Downton twenty-five minutes late, shortly before the arrival of 'Up' and 'Down' passenger trains. As the goods consisted of thirty-one vehicles and was almost twice the length of the passing loop, and no siding was available into which it could be shunted, the 'Up' passenger train could only pass, by the goods moving on to the single line north of the passing loop to enable the passenger to run in. When it was drawn up at the platform, the goods backed through on the 'Down' loop to the single line at the south end of the station to enable the passenger train to proceed to Salisbury.

The goods remained on the single line south of the station until the 'Down' passenger arrived when it then moved forward. Unfortunately Signalman Summers, in his effort not to delay the passenger train, failed to check that the tail lamps of the goods train were in place before lowering the signal to allow the passenger train to proceed. As it happened, when the goods started, the coupling between the sixteenth and seventeenth wagons broke allowing the rear 13 wagons and 2 brake vans to run backwards down the gradient of 1 in 78 before being stopped by Brakesman Ingram. The passenger train, which had by now accelerated to 20 m.p.h., struck those halted wagons, fortunately without causing serious injury to anyone.

Although the fault lay with Signalman Summers, some of the blame must be shared by Driver Dart and Guard Wisdom of the goods train. According to the rule book, Dart should have seen that, after starting, his fireman exchanged hand signals with the rear guard, and the front guard, Wisdom, should also have exchanged signals with the rear guard.

The Salisbury Market House Railway was a curious branch which, 510 yd in length, was the shortest independent standard-gauge line in Britain. The idea started back in 1856 when the Wilts., Somerset & Weymouth Railway, later taken over by the GWR, opened its branch from Westbury to Salisbury. The citizens of Salisbury, concerned in case their market died out because of the distance from the station, proposed a rail link. The Act, which received Royal Assent on 14 July 1856, permitted the Salisbury Railway & Market House Company to build a line and market, and raise a capital of £12,000 for this purpose.

The line was leased by the LSWR for £225 per annum, the rental being reduced to £112 11s. 0d. by 1896. At the time the agreement was arranged, the LSWR was constructing the direct line from Basingstoke. Most of the land required for the Market House Railway was not built on, but construction did require no less than four bridges along the line's short length – across two streams, the Avon, and the Mill Leat. The line was built by Thomas Brassey who charged £1,401 8s. 8d.

The Market House Railway opened on 24 May 1859. Despite its name, the market railway never carried meat, fish and poultry to market as was originally envisaged, but was principally concerned with taking coal and barley to the maltings which grew up on either side of the line; traffic to and from the saw mill; cheese; wool and seeds. In the period after the Second World War, coal for the Salisbury Electric Light & Supply Company, later part of the Southern Electricity Board, was the principal traffic. The power station changed to using oil fuel in 1962.

The Market House itself measured 77 ft by 174 ft, with walls of red and white brick and a glass roof. A gallery was provided for storing corn two sacks deep. The building's pedimented façade was in Bath stone. Provision was made for installing a clock to be given by the mayor, if the building was completed during his term of office. The structure cost £2,887.

The Market House was opened on 24 May 1859 with a celebratory dinner, followed by a concert given by the Band of the 1st Battalion of the City of Salisbury Rifle Corps. Within nine months of opening, sales of cheese, corn and wool, the commodities with which the building dealt, occupied all available space. The company paid its first dividend, 3½ per cent, in 1866. Subsequently 5 per cent was paid quite frequently until 1895 when revenue began to decline. The cheese traffic ceased in 1903, corn in 1913, while during the First World War the track inside the Market House was lifted. The seasonal wool market lasted until 1940 when only the corn market remained.

Despite the reduction of traffic, the company continued to pay respectable dividends –

5¼ per cent in 1933 and 12½ per cent in the 1950s. Latterly British Railways managed and worked the line at a rent of £150 per annum – £10 less than the LSWR charged ninety years previously! Following closure of the line on 1 July 1964, the track was lifted in December. The company was wound up by voluntary liquidation in 1965. The façade of the Market House building still remains, but the public library now occupies the site.

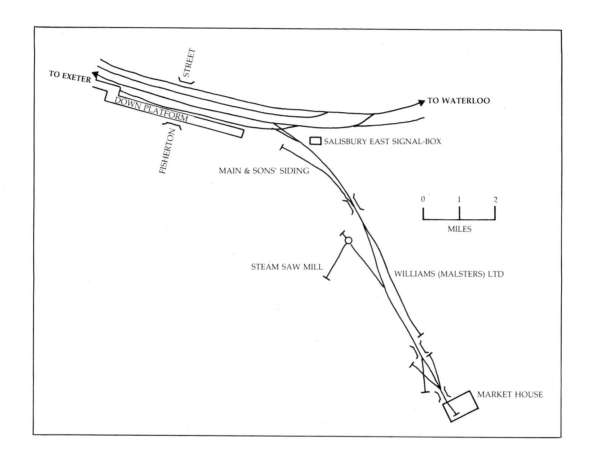

Ivatt class 2 2–6–2T No. 41320 shunting at Milford yard, Salisbury. The locomotive carries no headlamps or discs.

22.1.65 Paul Strong

Ivatt class 2 2–6–2T No. 41320, Milford yard, Salisbury.

22.1.65   Paul Strong

'Down' passenger train at Downton headed by Adams 0415 class 4–4–2T and consisting of six-wheel, six-compartment coaches. It is about to be crossed by an 'Up' train. The signal-box was subsequently reduced to a ground frame on 1 December 1922.

c. 1905   Lens of Sutton

An 'Up' train entering Downton.

c. 1905   Lens of Sutton

This view of Downton shows the former 'Down' loop which was converted into a siding 1 December 1922. The nearest wagon is an LMS vehicle, while the van belongs to the LNER. The cabin containing the ground frame can be seen below the centre of the footbridge.

c. 1930   Author's Collection

BR Standard Class 4 4–6–0 No. 75067 arriving at Downton with the 8.22 p.m. Salisbury to Bournemouth Central. The loop was not in use.

4.6.60   Hugh Ballantyne

Derailed coaches at the accident near Downton.

3.6.1884   *Graphic*

Derailed coaches near Downton.

3.6.1884   *Illustrated London News*

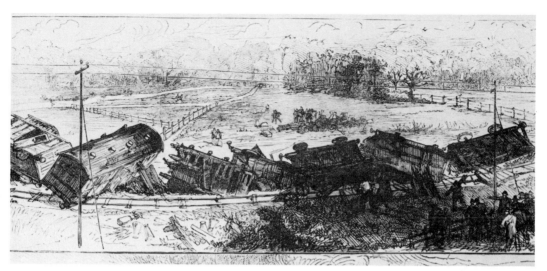

Rescuing the surviving passengers from the Downton accident.

3.6.1884   *Illustrated London News*

The Salisbury Market House. A railway wagon can just be seen behind the pillars on the left.

1859   *Illustrated London News*

The Military Branches:
Fovant Railway, Codford to
Codford Camp, and Heytesbury to
Sutton Veny Camp

Soon after the outbreak of war in 1914, work began on the construction of a line between Dinton and Fovant Camp. Until the railway's opening on 15 October 1915, transport between the station at Dinton and the camp was provided by traction engines which panted and wallowed in the mud. On 20 May 1916 the Commandant, Railway Training Centre, took over both operation and maintenance of the line which was worked by a varied selection of War Department locomotives. In the summer of 1916, Adams 4–4–2T No. 424 arrived. Surplus to London & South Western Railway requirements, she had stood outside Eastleigh Works since late 1913, the intention being to break her up, but with the outbreak of war, this was not proceeded with. Following repairs at Eastleigh where she was painted emerald green, lined out with gold and lettered 'Military Camp Railways No. 424'; she was initially sent to the Woolmer Instructional Military Railway before being transferred to Fovant. In October 1917 No. 424 suffered a derailment which caused the right-hand cylinder to be so badly damaged that another engine of the same class had to be cannibalized to provide a replacement. No. 424 continued to work on the Fovant line until closure when she was sent to Swindon for overhaul where she acquired a GWR polished safety valve cover before being despatched to Catterick Camp, Yorkshire.

Another engine which saw use on the Fovant line was *Westminster*, a Peckett 0–6–0ST, works No. 1378, built in 1914. As Military Camp Railways No. 13, painted holly green and decorated with polished brass and copper, it arrived on the line in 1917 after working at Bulford Camp. In later years it saw service at Shipton Cement Works, Oxfordshire, but is now preserved on the Kent & East Sussex Railway. Other locomotives which worked on the line at various times were: ex-Isle of Wight Railway No. 15 *Bembridge*, a Manning Wardle 0–6–0ST built in 1875 and used at Dinton from July 1916 until scrapped October 1920; No. 3 *Salisbury* and No. 4 *Seafield*, both Hudswell Clarke 0–6–0STs; No. 54, a Hudswell Clarke & Rogers 4–4–0T ex-Midland & Great Northern Railway which arrived in May 1917; *Codford*, a Hudswell Clarke 0–6–0ST from Sir John Jackson Limited's Codford Camp contract.

Kept very busy during the war, the camp's last job was dealing with demobilization. While this was in progress, a regular passenger service was run in addition to the many troop specials, the London & South Western Railway lending the carriages. Shunting operations at Dinton often seriously delayed regular trains on the main line and as a result, timekeeping suffered throughout the LSWR's West Country system.

The Fovant line closed on 18 December 1920, re-opened on 5 March 1921 and was finally taken out of use on 15 February 1924. The track was lifted about 1926, though its formation can yet be traced by the discerning eye, and ballast and the very occasional sleeper are still to be found in places.

The Fovant Military Railway ran from a trailing junction with the main LSWR's Salisbury to Exter line at Dinton. Branch trains used the south side of the 'Down' platform, crossed a red girder bridge over the River Nadder, went through Fovant Wood, passed over a level crossing, skirted Fir Hill keeping above the village, curved and ran approximately parallel with the A30 road towards Compton Chamberlayne where the large military camp was sited. The line was 2½ miles in length and had a ruling gradient of 1 in 35, which was steep for a railway.

To guard the main line from runaways, it was practice for a train from the camp to stop at a red light situated in front of the catch points just before the main line. When the train halted, and was therefore obviously under control, the catch point lever was pulled by the shunter, the points clipped to hold them in position for the train to pass safely over, and the train waved forward by a green flag by day, or a green light by night. Sometimes, to save effort, the points were not clipped, but merely held over.

On one such occasion, a train of Australian soldiers from the transit camp approached these catch points around midnight. They had spent the evening in a bout of heavy drinking prior to embarking for the Western Front and the chance of death. Their train was not provided with adequate toilet facilities, with the inevitable result that the shunter manning the catch points received an unexpected and unwelcome showerbath from the passing coach windows, soaking his uniform while he stuck dutifully to holding the catch points lever.

The track-lifting in 1926 was not quite the end of the story for this line. In 1937 it was decided to employ the disused limestone quarries, from which in previous centuries stone had been removed to build Salisbury Cathedral, to store RAF equipment. These caves in the woods were ideal, being deep underground, hidden from the air, yet accessible from the valley floor. From Dinton station a 2 ft gauge railway was laid to serve the dispersed sites, part of the route using an embankment and two bridges of the former Fovant Military Railway. The locomotives hauled rolling stock most of which was purpose-built on Hudson chassis dating from 1940. Because of the unlikely, but always possible, chance of a rock fall underground, six rescue wagons were always ready, as well as two fire tender wagons. Four permanent way wagons regularly patrolled the nine miles of track. Baguley-Drewry diesel locomotives were used on the surface and battery-electric locomotives by the same manufacturer underground. Earlier surface engines were Ruston & Hornsby diesels.

The Codford Camp line was another standard gauge military branch. It linked the GWR's Westbury to Salisbury line at Codford, with the camp 2¾ miles distant. The line connected with the 'Down' refuge siding at the west end of the station and curved northwards, climbing to the main road, now the A36. Runaways down this gradient to the station were not unknown.

The branch was built by Sir John Jackson Ltd and at least three locomotives were used in its construction: *Westminster*, a Peckett 0–6–0ST; *Codford*, a Hudswell, Clarke 0–4–0ST; and *Prince Edward*, a Manning Wardle 0–6–0T.

The line opened in October 1914, and an associated military platform with sidings at Codford was ready that same month. One of the engines which worked the new line was No. 16 *Finetta*, an Avonside 0–4–0ST from the Teign Valley Granite Co. Ltd, Devon.

141

It found post-war use at the Sandford Quarries, Banwell, Somerset owned by a subsidiary of the Teign Valley Granite Co. Ltd and was later transferred to yet another of that company's interests, Conygar Quarry, near Clevedon where it operated until rail traffic ceased *c.* 1935.

At the request of the War Department, the GWR took over working the Codford Camp line in May 1918. It is believed that GWR '517' class 0–4–2T No. 848 painted khaki, the standard GWR livery for that period, worked over the line. The Codford Camp line closed on 1 January 1923, and the track was removed the following year.

Yet another standard gauge military branch was that from Heytesbury, on the GWR's Westbury to Salisbury line, to Sutton Veny Camp. It was built by Oliver, Ling & Co., 1916–17 using No. 38 *Jersey Marine*, a Hunslet 0–6–0ST, this engine also working the completed line together with *Glasgow*, an Andrew Barclay 0–4–0ST. The branch served Sutton Veny Military Hospital, opened in 1916, which consisted of lines of huts on a mile-long site. It was constructed so that ambulance trains could conveniently draw up alongside the operating theatres.

Like the Codford Camp branch, the line was operated by the GWR from May 1918. Apart from a short length at the Heytesbury end, which remained as a siding until removal *c.* September 1935, the branch was closed and the track lifted by 1923.

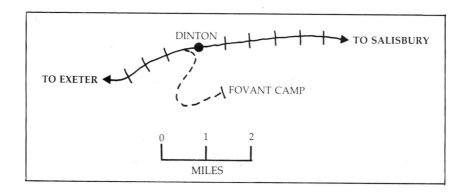

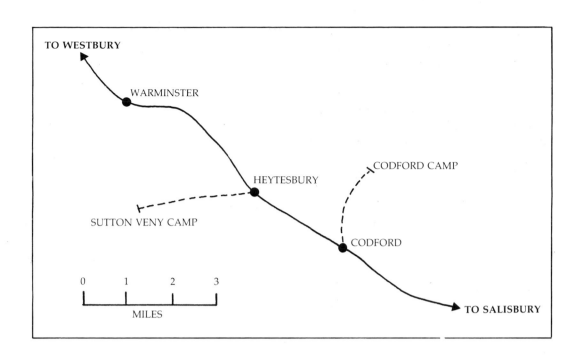

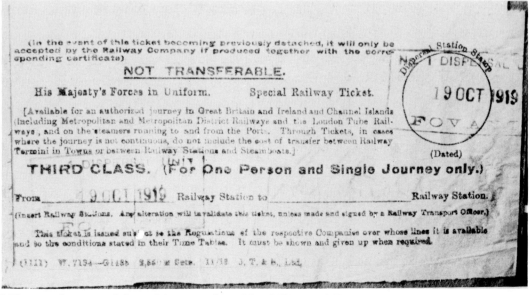

Military ticket issued for rail journey from No. 1 Dispersal Depot, Fovant, to Highbridge S&D station.

19.10.19   Author

A cutting of the Fovant Military Railway.

12.4.66   Author

RAF narrow-gauge passenger train running on the formation of the former Fovant Military Railway.

12.4.66   Author

A " War " Crowd at Codford Station.

The vast crew of workers who had been erecting Army huts at Codford Camp await a train home.
1915   *GWR Magazine*

Codford, note the bridge rail laid on the siding.

c. 1905   Author's Collection

'Castle' class No. 5080 *Defiant* piloting No. 4968 *Shotton Hall*, with the 5.02 p.m. Salisbury to Cardiff, the last train to call at Codford before the line was closed. It stopped on time at 5.30 p.m. and nine passengers got off. The points in the centre foreground at one time gave access to the line at Codford Camp.

17.9.55   Hugh Ballantyne